To learning professionals looking for a way to make all the pieces fit.
Your questions inspired me to look for answers.

WHAT WORKS IN TALENT DEVELOPMENT

| Blended Learning

Jennifer Hofmann

ATD Press is an internationally renowned source of insightful and practical information on talent development, training, and professional development.

ATD Press
1640 King Street
Alexandria, VA 22314 USA

Ordering information: Books published by ATD Press can be purchased by visiting ATD's website at www.td.org/books or by calling 800.628.2783 or 703.683.8100.

Library of Congress Control Number: 2017962658

ISBN-10: 1-56286-098-4
ISBN-13: 978-1-56286-098-1
e-ISBN: 978-1-56286-107-0

ATD Press Editorial Staff
Director: Kristine Luecker
Manager: Melissa Jones
Community of Practice Manager, Learning & Development: Amanda Smith
Developmental Editor: Jack Harlow
Text Design: Iris Sanchez and Francelyn Fernandez
Cover Design: Spencer Fuller, Faceout Studio, and Jason Mann

Printed by Data Reproductions Corporation, Auburn Hills, MI

Contents

About the Series

ATD's What Works in Talent Development series addresses the most critical topics facing today's talent development practitioners. Each book in the series is written for trainers, by trainers, and offers a clear and defined pathway to solving real issues. Interwoven with the latest findings in technology and best practices, this series is designed to enhance your current efforts on core subject matter, while offering a practical guide for you to follow. Authored by seasoned experts, each book is jam-packed with easy-to-apply content—including job aids, checklists, and other reference materials—to make the learning transfer process simple.

The What Works in Talent Development series is a unique core collection designed for talent development practitioners at every career level. To date, the books in the series include:

- *Starting a Talent Development Program*
- *Blending Learning*
- *Onboarding*

Introduction

Has your organization made blended learning a priority? Are you confused about what blended learning is, and how it can affect learning results? Perhaps you've seen many blended learning programs fail and want to make sure your initiative is successful. If you are involved with blended learning design in any way, or want to be, you need tools, resources, and a blueprint to move forward.

Whatever your situation, you've come to the right place to get started. This book is a good place to begin your journey—it will provide answers to many of your questions; but possibly more important, it poses additional questions that only you and your organization can answer. Answering these questions as you begin is crucial to ensure success. In addition, you'll benefit from the supplemental tools and worksheets designed to help you plan, design, implement, and evaluate blended learning campaigns.

Why Is Blended Learning Important?

Today, most learning is blended learning. Typically learning initiatives include some combination of live learning and self-directed learning, supported by resources like infographics, videos, and e-learning. But modern blended learning is more than sequencing different media and activities that happen to be related by topic. It is about aligning learning objects with the most appropriate instructional strategies, techniques, and technologies, while meeting the needs of the organization and modern learners.

When designed and implemented effectively, blended learning is very powerful. It creates individual resources that support formal, planned learning events, and supports every informal moment of learning need. An added benefit is that resources are no longer shelved or filed after the learning management system (LMS) has indicated completion; rather, they become crucial references and tools that learners can use far after the instructional program has ended.

Blended learning supports enhanced outreach to learners while connecting workforces that are globally dispersed, working virtually, and constantly on-the-go. In addition, blended learning resources are accessible to learners at the time and place of their convenience, as well as accommodating individuals with sight, hearing, and mobility impairments. Thus, blended learning makes your talent development initiatives more inclusive.

Blended learning also enables more authentic learning, by allowing individuals to learn, recall, and apply what they've learned when and where they need the content and perform their work. Blended learning campaigns, and their associated resources, provide the ability to create personal learning paths, allowing individuals to assess their own needs and make informed decisions about how and what to learn.

This book supports all members of the talent development community by providing insights on how to succeed in this potentially complex process.

Chapter by Chapter Overview

Each of the books in the What Works in Talent Development series follows a similar framework. The chapters in this book discuss what modern blended learning is, why it's important, how to design it, how to implement it, how to evaluate the outcome, and what you can do to prepare for the future of learning.

Chapter 1: Getting Started introduces modern blended learning by providing a clear definition of what constitutes blended learning today. It considers the changing perceptions around learning while providing insight into how to assess your situation and ways to evaluate your current learning landscape. A new role is proposed to lead the change: the learning experience architect.

Because so much of modern blended learning is new, this chapter also includes a list of key terms to help you to manage blended learning conversations with your stakeholders. You'll be introduced to the concept of a learning campaign, which can replace the more traditional course model. Learning campaign design and implementation is a foundational concept that supports the rest of the book. It also ties together the five moments of learning need: when learning something new, when learning more, when applying what was learned, when solving problems, and when things change.

Chapter 1 asks you to consider many questions: What is the history and the future of blended learning at your organization? What is the current perception, and how can you shape it? How do you currently address all the moments of learning need? What is your role in moving forward with blended learning initiatives?

You will also find tools that allow you to reflect on past blended learning efforts, create learner personas, and start to build your personal learning network.

Chapter 2: Shaping the Future helps you set the stage for success. For blended learning to be successful, it is necessary to lay a strong foundation to manage the change from more traditional models.

This chapter addresses the migration from a "push training model," where learners are assigned content as determined by business needs, to a "pull learning model," where learners are enabled to learn how, where, and when they want to. It provides strategies for talent development to partner with the business and with learners to help the organization progress along the change curve.

Critical in this chapter is the discussion about where modern learning takes place (in a traditional classroom, at a desk, on a mobile device, or on the job) and how it takes place (formally or informally). These critical aspects determine how the learning programs should be designed, and help create a more authentic learning environment. We also discuss the application of adult learning principles, which is more important than ever.

Chapter 2 asks you to think about what surprised you about the design, cost, and instructional complexity of past blended learning initiatives. Other questions include how globalization, mobilization, and social collaborative technologies affect your campaign design. Should they? How do you make reusable individual learning resources, potentially supporting all the moments of learning need? How can you learn from problems with the design, technology, and implementation of early initiatives to mitigate future issues?

This chapter provides a job aid to help you plot where your organization is on the change curve. A list of additional resources rounds out this chapter.

Chapter 3: Designing Your Blended Learning Program addresses how to design modern blended learning campaigns. Instructional design is critical to blended learning, and arguably more important than ever before. As with more traditional methods, blended learning campaign design starts with a needs assessment. This process links learning outcomes to business requirements, and identifies whether your organization is ready for this type of implementation.

This chapter distinguishes the difference between instructional strategies that provide the framework for learning (game-based learning, problem-based learning, task-based learning), instructional techniques that are used to implement the strategy (lecture, brainstorm, gamification, simulations, and other activities), and instructional technologies that are used to deploy the techniques (authoring tools, virtual classrooms, and other technology). The key takeaway here is that technology selection is the last part of the design process, not the first.

It can be difficult for everyone, including the design team, learners, and other stakeholders, to navigate the instructional complexity of a blended learning campaign. We'll discuss how using a course map can help, and you'll learn how to create one.

Questions addressed in this chapter include, "What role does collaboration play in technology selection?" "How ready is your organization to accept blended learning?" "How ready are you?" "Can you link your design directly to your business needs?"

These are tough questions, and it's up to you to provide the answers within your organization. To support your effort, you'll find a business requirements worksheet; a blended learning organizational readiness assessment; an instructional technology inventory worksheet; a tool to assist you in mapping your learning objectives to instructional strategies, techniques, and technologies; and a job aid to help you create your course map. A list of additional resources rounds out this chapter.

Chapter 4: Implementing the Plan assists you in making your design a functional reality. It's critical to have a way to manage all these moving parts and different content types. The content strategy plan addresses content substance, structure, workflow, and governance.

You also need a plan to facilitate your blended learning campaign. The facilitator is the face of the campaign, responsible for managing live virtual classroom lessons, moderating social experiences, supporting self-directed lessons, curating content, and providing virtual coaching and mentoring. This chapter suggests a team approach: using a facilitator and a producer together to motivate learners, encourage collaboration, manage technology, and ensure a successful learning experience.

Modern blended learning campaigns should evolve as new content and ideas are introduced; this requires the curation of content. Implementing a content curation plan that can inform and engage all learners around the topic is a way for the entire organization to stay up to date. It enables a culture of perpetual learning, and supports the modern workplace learning mindset that encourages learners to pursue independent learning and create their own personal learning paths. But managers are still vital to ensuring organizational buy-in, so this chapter provides guidance on how to engage managers in blended learning early.

Chapter 4 asks you to consider: What is your current process for content life cycle maintenance, and how might it need to change? What is the role of facilitation in your current strategy, and will it change? How do you currently engage managers in learning?

Tools to support your effort include a content strategy planning tool, a content curation planning tool, and a blended learning implementation plan worksheet.

Chapter 5: Transferring Learning and Evaluating Results discusses the particulars of how to evaluate a blended learning campaign. Design and implementation of blended learning is focused on planning—and the same should apply to evaluation. Blended learning campaigns introduce evaluation challenges that simply don't exist when assessing traditionally delivered programs.

You start the evaluation process by answering the question, "What does success look like and how will I recognize it when it happens?" This chapter helps you to identify the answer. You also need to determine what types of data should be collected, and how often.

Learner engagement is critical to the success of a blended learning campaign. This chapter provides a framework for measuring engagement across three factors: the emotional, intellectual, and environmental response to the campaign.

This chapter asks you to consider how you evaluate learner success today, and what you do with those data. Do you currently measure engagement? How do they change your design? Do you use all the data you collect?

Tools to support your effort include a worksheet to measure the three factors of learner engagement, a blended learning instructional design effective practice scorecard, and a tool for the learner to evaluate the facilitator, producer, and themselves.

Chapter 6: Planning Next Steps wraps up the book and includes topics that address the question, "Now what?" You will explore recommendations to ensuring ongoing success for blended learning campaign implementation in your organization. This chapter also reminds you to provide the right content, in the right place, at the right time, to the right audience. To assist with adoption, implement a marketing campaign and partner with managers. Use past evaluation results to help shape future campaigns.

Chapter 6 also envisions the future of blended learning. Personal learning pathways will provide laser-focused content to learners. Technologies like xAPI will allow you to measure engagement and learning more exactly. And new approaches like immersive learning and user-generated content will create experiences you couldn't even imagine five years ago.

This chapter, and this book, concludes by encouraging you to design a personal blended learning campaign to help you stay ahead of new trends and techniques.

Tools to support your effort include a blended learning marketing plan worksheet, a checklist of items to include in your blended learning campaign orientation, a learning pathway planning worksheet, and a list of experts to help you start your personal learning network.

How to Get the Most Out of This Book

Blended Learning gets you started on the path to designing and implementing blended learning campaigns. It is meant to be a guide and overview for the topic. It is not meant to be an all-encompassing reference for instructional design, evaluation, or instructional technologies. The book provides enough information to get you started, as well as the tools and tips you need to head in the right direction. However, to be successful you'll need to incorporate the nuances of your organization and its particular needs. This book cannot cover every possible option, so be sure to tap into the resources provided in each chapter to take your exploration and deliberation to the next level.

And don't learn in a vacuum. Modern blended learning may be new to you and others in your organization; use this book to learn together so you can support your organization and your learners.

Chances are, you won't use every resource right away. That's OK. Modern blended learning supports every moment of your personal learning need—not just when you are learning something new. Refer to the individual tools when you need them.

This book is just one part of your personal learning journey. Share what you've learned with your learning networks, and become part of the way we'll all learn in the future.

Icons Used in This Book

Throughout this book, you'll find icons highlighting concepts and ideas introduced in the text.

Icon	What It Means
💡	*Tips from professionals* will make your job easier and give you ideas to help apply the techniques and approaches discussed.
🛠	*Tools* identify templates, checklists, worksheets, models, outlines, examples, illustrations, and other prototypes that can be a useful place to start.
🔍	*Resources* are the books, blogs, articles, or even people that you can access to add to the information you've gained already and take your learning deeper.

1

Getting Started: What Is Blended Learning?

In This Chapter

- A definition of blended learning
- Ideas for assessing your situation
- A look at the changing perceptions around learning
- Who should lead the change to blended learning

Many practitioners have thought of blended learning as three-dimensional in the way it incorporates instructional treatments, leverages educational technologies, and occurs in different places. And yet the modern blend is more than what, how, and where people are learning. It's also about when people are learning. The fact is, modern learners are learning all the time—modern blended learning is actually four-dimensional.

Supported by job aids, worksheets, and curated resources, we will explore what works for modern blended learning. Use this book as your starting point in your personal learning path to blended learning.

Defining Blended Learning

Blended learning is a series of content blocks sequenced to create learning experiences. This is a managed, trackable curriculum with a beginning and an end. You, the learning professional, match learning objectives to the most appropriate delivery medium and learning environment to ensure that participants learn through facilitator-led delivery of content while exerting some element of control over where, when, how fast, and so on.

In addition to this formal learning experience, blended learning also includes those experiences that happen outside a formal curriculum. Learning designers need to keep in mind that learning is perpetual, happening all around your learners. This book will consider the entire experience, and address how you can support learners in every moment of learning need.

Modern Classrooms

Today's classroom isn't just a place—it's an experience. Modern learning happens in the traditional classroom, on a mobile device, at a desk, and on the job. These places of learning can include a wide number of learning technologies, and lend themselves to either formal or informal learning events. However, just because someone can learn in a particular place doesn't necessarily mean it's the most authentic learning environment.

The modern workforce is more dispersed yet more interconnected than ever before. Organizational learning is not just designed to provide information; its goal is to help learners become better at their jobs. When you design training, you need to take the audience into consideration and create programs that reflect the global, social, and mobile nature of work.

Modern Design

Instructional design for blended learning must be rigorously applied. Poor or ineffective design becomes much more apparent when the learner is exposed to a variety of instructional treatments that can't be "made OK" by an instructor in the room. The big question in a blended solution is how to know when to use which technique or technology—hardly a day goes by without some new theory or treatment being touted as the harbinger of groundbreaking change that will redefine how you instruct, learn, or assess.

One of the earliest examples of this phenomena dates back to Thomas Edison in 1913, when discussing motion pictures:

> The motion picture is the great educator of the poorer people. It incites their imagination by bringing the whole world before their eyes. It sets spectators thinking and raises their standard of living. Books will soon be obsolete in the public schools. Scholars will be instructed through the eye. It is possible to teach every branch of human knowledge with the motion picture. Our school system will be completely changed inside of ten years. (Keegan 2013, 145)

It's interesting to note that, more than 100 years later, people are still looking to video as the answer to all things in learning.

A more recent example is the introduction of MOOCs (massive open online courses). The *New York Times* declared 2012 "The Year of the MOOC" (Pappano 2012). But by 2015, the excitement abated:

> Three years after a groundswell of online learning swept through higher education, Stanford researchers who were at the forefront of the movement have concluded that online learning has not been the cure-all that many educators had hoped for. (Stober 2015)

The latest "game changer" is the emergence of the Experience API (xAPI) software, which allows content, like e-learning and video, to send information to learning management systems. It is intended to track engagement with learners and learning experiences, and is touted as "the future of learning" by facilitating the way we create and manage learning worldwide. The next several years will show if this latest innovation stands up to the hype.

New research into instructional tools, techniques, and technology helps to advance the profession, but the results and their interpretation generally leave a learning professional with little idea how to apply them, not to mention how to leverage them strategically to connect all the learning objectives in a blended learning curriculum. Instead, to facilitate understanding, it's useful to group concepts into three categories: instructional strategies, instructional techniques, and instructional technologies. While certainly not the only method of classification, organizing them in this way permits a meaningful discussion of blended learning. Here are the questions each category addresses.

Instructional Strategies

What instructional strategy should be used to help learners achieve the desired level of mastery for that specific learning objective? When you choose an instructional strategy, you choose an overall approach for addressing the instructional need: It frames the approach that you will subsequently populate with a variety of techniques and technologies to achieve your instructional objective. In some ways, the instructional strategy is based on fundamental characteristics of the learning audience and the content. Instructional strategies include game-based learning, social collaborative learning, problem-based learning, self-directed learning, case-based learning, and task-based instruction.

Instructional Techniques

What technique should be used to implement the instructional strategy? Techniques support the strategy, and generally can be thought of as peers—that is, you can substitute one technique with another, and the learner outcome should be the same. This is not to say that two techniques applied to the same content (say self-paced computer-based instruction versus traditional in-person) produce an equivalent experience, but the incremental progress the learner makes toward the overall instructional objective is the same. Instructional techniques frame the approach to how the learner will progress through the instruction, and they include simulations, curated learning environments, learning communities, gamification, case studies, moderated discussions, and lectures.

Instructional Technologies

What technologies and tools should be used to support the method? Technologies include authoring and delivery tools, and are used to deploy an instructional method. Lectures (a method) can be deployed in a traditional or virtual classroom, by video, or even by podcast (the technology). The technology selection will be determined largely on assessment and evaluation requirements. It will also be affected by where learners are when they apply the skill or need the knowledge, to ensure learning is deployed in the most authentic way possible.

TOOLS

Throughout this book, I will refer to these concepts as strategy, technique, and technology. To help you recall the difference between them when it's time to design your blended learning curriculum, refer to the "Instructional Strategies, Techniques, and Technologies" tool at the end of this chapter.

As blended learning becomes the norm, the hurdles you face will become more complicated. For example, tracking learning completion and mastery poses a serious logistical concern. You'll need to answer questions about how, and if, to measure engagement with infographics, videos, books and blogs, and social learning communities. Do you measure each interaction and engagement, or the entire experience? (This is the problem xAPI is intended to solve.)

You are going to have to do a lot of work to set yourself up for success. It's going to require you to design, deliver, and prepare content for learners, and understand all the available tools and techniques.

Modern Integration

For any blended learning solution to be effective, you need to be able to integrate many concepts into one cohesive program. The flexibility and options for blend can make this even more difficult than if you only used one type of training approach. In addition to being able to build content in authoring tools, moderate discussions, motivate learners, and manage a blended learning implementation, you need to understand how instructional technologies and strategies are interrelated.

This is challenging. New instructional strategies—curation, game-based learning, and social collaborative learning—are very different from traditional design strategies. Technologies are being introduced and phased out all the time.

Learning professionals tend to master these concepts in silos. You might attend a webinar on how to curate. You might take a course on how to facilitate in the virtual classroom. You might purchase a book on microlearning. That's great, but the problem is that cross-training rarely exists. How do you gamify the virtual classroom? Can you use microlearning during a simulation? Does a makerspace work on a mobile device?

The point of asking these questions is to illustrate that a true blended learning program doesn't keep its ingredients separate. When designing a blend, you combine instructional strategies, techniques, and technologies with your knowledge about the modern learning landscape to create a product that balances the needs of learners with the requirements of the business.

Assessing Your Blended Learning Situation

Let's start with an assumption: Today, all learning is blended to some degree. I challenge you to identify any truly impactful program that doesn't combine facilitator-led and learner-led activities. Traditional classroom programs usually include pre-work and suggestions for follow-up activities. Lessons delivered virtually are often supported by videos and e-learning. Even content designed as a standalone module, such as an animated video demonstrating how to create a formula in a spreadsheet, works on the assumption that the learner will independently practice the new skill until the desired level of mastery is achieved.

Learning professionals influence the designed experiences, such as e-learning and traditional classroom programs. But as you assess the business requirements for training solutions, you also need to consider those experiences that are not designed—those experiences that are more learner-directed. Sure, you can assume that someone who completes an e-learning module will practice the skill, but why stop there? You can influence the mastery of that skill by offering guidance on how to practice, providing curated resources so they can learn more, and building reminders that encourage learners to continue toward mastery.

Instead of assessing whether you need a blended learning solution, let's investigate the true learning need. This starts with taking an inventory of what you already have.

Learning Landscape

Whether you are starting to design a specific blended learning program or creating a strategic plan for your talent development department, you need to know what's worked in the past, what resources are available, who your learners are, and how prepared your organization is to accept a modern blended learning design.

History

Even if your organization is just starting to create formal blended learning for the first time, you should research how different delivery methods and instructional treatments have worked in the past. It's important to understand that modern blended learning is a major change in the way that organizations traditionally deliver content. And, it affects much more than just the learner population; you need to consider where the entire organization is on the change curve. Chapter 2 will provide strategies for encouraging the adoption of blended learning through the four stages of change: denial, resistance, exploration, and commitment.

Use evaluation data or LMS reports to determine how well different initiatives were received and how influential they were on learning outcomes and performance.

Don't forget the human element. Interview designers, learners, project sponsors, and anyone else who was involved to get a full picture of what has worked in the past and what has not. Make sure you get to the "why." If it didn't work, was the reason technology, a reluctance to adopt, lack of sponsorship, or just a bad idea? Make sure you document what you've learned, so your entire organization can learn from previous successes and failures.

TOOL

At the end of this chapter, you'll find the "Reflection on Past Blended Learning Efforts" tool, which can guide your reflection on past blended learning implementations. Use this informal tool at the beginning of every new project so you can capitalize on past successes and avoid past mistakes.

Resources

Before you start designing a blended learning curriculum, it's critical that you know what resources are already available to you. Research the following:

- What delivery technologies and authoring tools has your organization already invested in, and how can you get access to those tools? (Chapter 3 will discuss six different categories of learning technologies, and provide a checklist to help you take inventory of what your organization does and doesn't have.)
- Who knows how to use those tools?
- Do you use internal resources or external suppliers?
- Is there training available for you to gain some new skill sets?
- Do you have the time to learn?

It's important to remember that you are not an inexhaustible resource on this team, and, depending on the instructional complexity of your blend, chances are you don't have the expertise to complete the entire project, or the time to get it done, on your own.

PRO TIP

If you are working on a small or one-person team, you need to plan accordingly. Perhaps you have the skills to design, develop, and moderate the entire initiative, but you will probably need more time to roll out the program.

When you design your blend, critically evaluate if you have the resources to be successful. If not, consider what is critical right away and what might be developed in later versions. A simple design that is successful is ultimately much more valuable than a complex design that fails.

Learner Profiles

Engaging your learners takes more than content and technology. You need to know who your learners are; in effect, you need to design your programs with *personas* in mind. Don't assume that because someone is a salesperson, for example, you understand that learner's persona. When you create a persona, think about the learner's individual needs, and how those needs intersect with their professional development goals. What's their existing skill set, and how do you expect them to behave in a certain scenario? Each profile will include background on the persona, including where they're doing their job, what education level they have, their experience with training and education in general, and as much other detail as you can include. The better you know your learner, the better your blended learning program will be. See the sidebar for an example of a call center representative's learner persona.

TOOL

At the end of this chapter, you'll find a worksheet to help you create your own learner personas.

Call Center Representative Learner Persona

Mandy is always eager to meet the needs of her customers. She consistently puts the customers first and does her best to make them feel appreciated. Mandy believes that customers prefer to speak to a human being, so she avoids suggesting the use of the website quick reference and FAQs. She thrives on fostering consulting-type relationships with the client base, and would prefer to talk with the customers than tell them to use self-service applications. She has had formal training on how to deal with difficult customers and was often brought in on calls that other representatives could not manage.

Age: 45

Education: Undergraduate degree in social science

Prior work history: 10 years of experience in customer service for a large pharmaceutical company

Learner preparation: Mandy is eager to start this new position, and has carefully read through everything she could find about the company and services provided. She went as far as to call in to the service desk to see what the experience is like.

Technology preferences: Mandy uses a laptop computer at home, and carries an Android smartphone with her. She uses the phone mostly for calls, and games.

Challenges and obstacles: Mandy is hesitant to embrace web-based resources and does not consider herself tech-savvy.

Learning Need

According to Sardek Love (2016), "Failure to invest sufficient time to properly define the problem almost always results in providing a solution to the wrong problem." Creating a blended learning solution is a lot of work, potentially expensive, and, when not done for the right reasons, can leave a lasting negative impression of the value of blended learning in an organization. Because of this, it's critical that you conduct a training needs analysis before building your blended learning solution. It needs to meet both the needs of the learner and the needs of the business.

This shouldn't be a surprise. Conducting a needs analysis should be the first step in the design of any training program. Here are five phases to consider when conducting a needs assessment:

- **Organizational Needs:** Identify and validate organizational goals.
- **Performance Needs:** Identify gaps between current and desired performance, including the causes for those performance gaps.

- **Performer Needs:** Identify existing learner knowledge.
- **Potential Solutions:** Identify learning and nonlearning solutions.
- **Findings and Recommendations:** Present a final report that frames data, results, and recommendations.

PRO TIP

Your needs assessment for the blended learning program will likely overlap with those for other programs and possibly uncover the same information. Meet a colleague for coffee and compare your results. You will minimize duplication of efforts, and make your insights even more useful.

Blended learning requires you to be even more specific when identifying performance needs and performer needs. (As a result, you may have more specific potential solutions.) That's because with modern blended learning design, you can be responsive not just when learners are learning something new for the first time; you can design and implement solutions that affect every moment of learning need.

Conrad Gottfredson and Bob Mosher (2012) identified five moments of learning need to help illustrate where performance support could supplement the formal learning process. These same moments lend themselves to the entire blended learning process, because different training solutions support different moments of need. These moments are:

- when people are learning how to do something for the first time (new)
- when people are expanding the breadth and depth of what they have learned (more)
- when people need to act upon what they have learned, which includes planning what they will do, remembering what they may have forgotten, or adapting their performance to a unique situation (apply)
- when problems arise, or things break or don't work the way they were intended (solve)
- when people need to learn a new way of doing something, which requires them to change skills that are deeply ingrained in their performance practices (change).

Chapter 3 will address how to meet these moments of need during the formal blended learning campaign and after the formal program has concluded.

RESOURCES

The neuroscience of learning shows that a training-as-an-event model lets organizations down and leaves learners scratching their heads. To embrace all that learners need to support their performance on the job, Megan Torrance expanded Conrad Gottfredson and Bob Mosher's five moments to nine. Although all nine moments may not be relevant to every project, they provide a framework for thinking about multiple touchpoints with the learner over time. See Megan's *TD* article "Nine Moments for Learning" for more information (www.td.org/magazines/td-magazine/nine-moments-of-learning).

Changing Perceptions

It won't come as a surprise to you that some elements of learning initiatives aren't taken seriously by the learner population. Webinars are considered hour-long, listen-only events. Learners don't consider them to be as effective as face to face, and the recording has the same value as the live session. Pre-work is considered optional, and rarely completed.

In addition, everyone, learners and training team members alike, overly focus on the "most live" part of the training curriculum. For example, if presented with a blend that includes e-learning modules, a virtual classroom session, a two-day workshop, and a variety of follow-up activities, the focus will be on the two-day workshop. Communication will focus on logistics of getting there, and the learners will view any self-directed work as optional. After all, if it was really important, the content would be delivered in the classroom.

For blended learning to be successful, these perceptions need to change. Every part of a blend—regardless of delivery technology (like virtual classroom, video, or infographic) or instructional strategy (like microlearning, social-collaborative learning, or simulation)—needs to be considered important. Chapter 2 will consider change management strategies in more depth, but for now you need to start by establishing some new labels for the different components of a blend.

Words matter, especially when trying to communicate new ideas and teach new concepts. Terms like microlearning, virtual classrooms, and mobile learning aren't enough to encompass what you are trying to accomplish, and, frankly, don't mean anything to your learners. The goal of modern blended learning is to integrate content, exercises, and assessment into a seamless curriculum, regardless of what delivery technologies or instructional strategies are used. To accommodate this goal, you need to embrace a subtle shift in language when designing blended learning experiences. And because an individual lesson will often be part of a larger learning solution, the language shift applies to all modern learning, independent of the learning environment.

Modern workplace learning is more than technology. It's about changing the way you think about how modern learners actually learn. Adopting a language that supports this new way of thinking is a great way to start. Throughout this book, I'll be using the following terms:

- **Session:** A standalone presentation, webinar, interactive e-learning module, or similar unit that has no associated assessments or required actions. The intent of a session is to share information and provide opportunities for basic interactions to ensure understanding.

- **Lesson:** When the audience is actively learning something new, with an expectation that there will be some assessment (either a formal test or self-assessment) to ensure that knowledge has been transferred or skills obtained. A lesson is characterized by practice: If the learner doesn't have the opportunity to do something with the content, it is not a lesson. It can be delivered through a virtual classroom, with an e-learning module, in person, or using many other technologies. The word *lesson* makes all content in a blend equal, and it shifts the focus from the delivery technology to the content, because learners are not distracted by tech speak.

- **Practice Activity:** The opportunity to practice or use content obtained during a lesson. The activity can be collaborative or self-led.

- **Assessment:** An evaluation or checkpoint that ensures the learning has been transferred. It can be a traditional multiple-choice type test or on-the-job observation; embedded as a moderated activity, like group work; or self-directed, like a reflection activity.

- **Resource:** Reinforces, reminds, or introduces content. It is reusable, and should be designed as a performance support tool. Resources include infographics, short videos, podcasts, social collaborative communities, and coaching—anything that supports the learning before and after the formal event.

- **Content Block:** You might also call this a "chunk" of learning. A content block is a group of integrated lessons, activities, assessments, and resources that, when combined, support an individual learning objective or goal.

- **Learning Campaign:** More and more frequently, the term blended learning isn't descriptive enough, especially when you consider that learning takes place perpetually, even when the training department isn't looking. To become more of a partner with your business, you need make sure learning opportunities and content are where and when your learners need them. A learning campaign extends the learning beyond formal events.

- **Perpetual Learning:** While this term sounds a lot like lifelong learning, it's more nuanced. It takes into consideration that everything we do, in every waking moment, is, or can be, an opportunity to learn. Every time we read an article, click a link, or complete a task, we are learning something new or practicing and reinforcing a skill. Sometimes it is conscious, sometimes unconscious. But it is still learning. You need to find ways to encourage, support, and anticipate perpetual learning in the content, interaction, and assessment areas you manage.

- **Learning Experience Architect:** This individual is the project manager for modern blended learning implementation. Learning experience architects constantly improve the learning experience through design and implementation, all while balancing the demands of the business with modern learners' needs. This individual needs to understand design, development, facilitation, curation, and a lot more. The learning experience architect must be able to discuss the business of learning, evaluate delivery technologies and instructional strategies, and stay ahead of trends in the industry.

Leading the Change

Who should lead the movement to blended learning? It's an evolution of the traditional L&D role—learning professionals are already expected to be masters of traditional learning roles, including developer, facilitator, and designer. Combine this with the expectation that learning professionals are also producers, moderators, curators, and learner advocates, and it becomes clear that the job is not only important but complicated. The ultimate responsibility is to provide the correct content, to the correct audience, at the appropriate time. Given how many of us came to learning through other professions, this is a herculean task.

Because of this, I've adopted a new title to best represent the professional responsible for workplace learning: learning experience architect (Seitzinger 2016). Learning experience architects constantly improve the learning experience through design and implementation, all while balancing the demands of the business with modern learners' needs, and managing the change process.

RESOURCES

To learn more about becoming a learning experience architect and reimagining your role, read "The Learning Experience Architect: Reimagining Your Role" on the InSync Training blog. (You can access it at http://bit.ly/2iwUDq2.)

To establish credibility as an expert in blended learning approaches, the learning experience architect should develop at least a working competence in the following areas:

- **The business of learning:** Being able to balance the requirements of the business with the needs of your learners enables you to become a valued business adviser who can address important issues such as the ROI of training, measurement and evaluation, project planning, and organizational needs.

- **Instructional strategies, technologies, and techniques:** Determining whether new approaches like simulations or social collaboration are good for your audience can be a struggle for even seasoned learning professionals. It's typical to inconsistently apply new techniques like gamification, and then discard them for the next big thing. The learning experience architect must be fluent in the language of modern instructional design to make the best decisions and communicate effectively with the rest of the implementation team and stakeholders.

- **Collaboration:** Today's learners are more connected than ever through social media and their mobile devices. Collaboration needs to be strategically implemented in your blended learning designs, so that it is valued by the learners. To develop competence in effective collaboration, learning experience architects can make connections and participate in communities of practice. Immersing yourself in collaborative experiences will help you make informed recommendations to your learners.

- **Educational technology trends:** When it comes to new learning trends, learning experience architects understand that knowing what's hot now is just half the battle. If you can find out "what's next," you'll establish yourself as a partner to the business, and make sure that working and learning are never far apart.

By establishing the learning experience architect as the individual in charge of blended learning adoption, modern design expertise, and the business of learning (among so many other things), the organization can show its commitment to blended learning as a valued learning experience.

Training the Team

Part of your change plan needs to include reskilling your training team. Consider that any individual might be called on to moderate social collaborative experiences, curate learning resources, author e-learning or video content, facilitate in virtual classrooms, or manage a blended learning implementation. Trying to successfully implement a blend without experienced human resources can put a halt to your initiative before it even starts.

Whenever possible, encourage the training team to develop these skills before it becomes critical. Research learning options and help individuals create their own personal learning paths so they can be successful. By encouraging members of your team to develop new skill sets to help them master the design, development, and implementation of blended learning, you will assist them along the change curve. This investment in their professional development is an investment in the success of the business.

TOOL

Looking for some resources that support your professional development? Check out the "Build Your Personal Learning Network" tool at the end of this chapter.

What's Next?

How do you know if your blended learning campaign has been successful? While chapter 4 will discuss the specifics of how you evaluate each content block, the technology, the facilitation team, and learner success, it's still an important point to contemplate when you're getting started.

You will know whether the program is successful if you've continued to ask questions throughout the process and paid close attention to learner engagement, facilitator involvement, assessment results, and so on. As your blended learning campaign becomes more and more instructionally complex, it becomes even more critical not to wait to the end to take a pulse and evaluate your success up to that point.

It's important to understand that if you're not paying attention and your blended learning design falls apart, learners may recognize the failure days, weeks, or even months before you do. Don't make the mistake of just paying attention to the "live" event. You need to connect the dots between all your content, anticipating what your learners need and ensuring they have access to that content at the right time.

There's another important reason why you can't wait until the end of your blend to evaluate your success: Modern blended learning never ends. Even after you close the books in the LMS, learning continues. So another barometer of success is that the tools and content you provided during the formal program are accessed months later, and recognized by the learners as useful and worth their time. Remember, modern learners are learning perpetually, in every moment of learning need. The job of the talent development professional is to anticipate and support this perpetual learning cycle (Figure 1-1).

Figure 1-1. Perpetual Learning

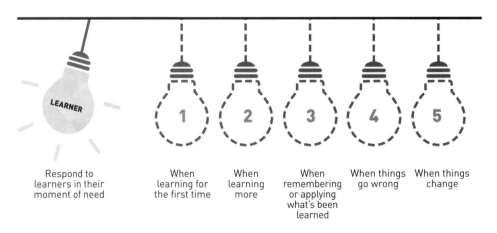

Questions to Explore

- What does your organization consider to be the future of learning? Do you agree?
- How do globalization and mobilization affect your learning audience and content design?
- Aside from language and culture concerns, what are barriers to success in your organization?
- What is the history of blended learning implementation in your organization? Have past failures thrown up difficult barriers? How will you keep blended learning from seeming like the next fad?
- What moments of learning need did your last training program address? What moments were overlooked? Can you address them now, embedding them in the flow of work?
- What learning terms in your organization bring on a negative reaction? How can you change the perception, or change the word completely, to get a better response from your learners and other key stakeholders?
- As you work toward becoming a learning experience architect, how do your learning needs align with those of your learners? How can you use that to your advantage when designing blended learning?
- What does blended learning success mean to you? How will you recognize it?

Tools for Support

Instructional Strategies, Techniques, and Technologies

Instructional design for modern blended learning must be rigorously applied, anticipate the correct moments of learning need, and embed content in the flow of work. To facilitate understanding and permit meaningful discussion in the context of blended learning, it's useful to group concepts into three categories: strategies, techniques, and technologies. Use this job aid to help you recall the difference between these concepts when it's time to design your blended learning curriculum.

Instructional Strategies	Instructional Techniques	Instructional Technologies
Instructional strategies are the overall approach for addressing the instructional need—they frame the approach that you will subsequently populate with a variety of techniques and technologies to achieve your instructional objective. In some ways, the instructional strategy is based on fundamental characteristics of the nature of both the learning audience and the content.	Instructional techniques support the strategy, and generally can be thought as peers of each other— that is, you can substitute one technique with another, and the learner outcome should be the same (although the experience will vary extensively). Instructional techniques frame the approach on how the learner will progress through the instruction.	Technology selection will be determined largely on assessment and evaluation requirements. It will also be affected by where learners are when they are applying the skill or need the knowledge; you want to deploy learning in the most authentic way possible.

Instructional Strategies	Instructional Techniques	Instructional Technologies
What instructional strategies do you plan to use to help learners achieve the desired level of mastery for your learning objective? (Check as many as apply.) ☐ Task-based learning ☐ Game-based learning ☐ Social collaborative learning ☐ Problem-based learning ☐ Project-based learning ☐ Inquiry-based learning ☐ Case-based learning ☐ Other: _____	What instructional techniques do you plan to use to implement the instructional strategy? (Check as many as apply.) ☐ Lectures (live, recorded, or print on screen) ☐ Brainstorming between learners ☐ Simulations (including role play and immersive learning) ☐ Gamification (including leader boards and badging) ☐ Case studies (including examples that illustrate key points) ☐ Moderated discussion boards (including in-person discussions and online) ☐ Other: _____	What technologies and tools do you plan to use to support the instructional techniques? (Check as many as apply.) ☐ Knowledge and content distribution ☐ Communication and interaction ☐ Social interactions, collaboration, and community ☐ Assessment and evaluation ☐ Immersive learning experiences ☐ Curation ☐ Other: _____

Reflection on Past Blended Learning Efforts

These questions can help guide your reflection of past blended learning implementations. Use this informal tool at the beginning of every new project so you can capitalize on previous successes and avoid past mistakes.

What is the history of blended learning implementation in your organization?
- What delivery methods and instructional treatments have worked in the past?
- Why were they successful?
- What delivery methods and instructional treatments have NOT worked in the past?
- Why were they unsuccessful? (Was it technology related, reluctance to adopt, lack of sponsorship, or just a bad idea?)

How prepared is your organization to accept a modern blended learning design?
- Who are your learners?
- What resources are available?
- Where is the organization on the change curve?
- Have past failures thrown up difficult barriers? If so, what are those barriers?

How will you keep blended learning from seeming like the next fad?

Creating a Learner Persona

Learner Name	
[Learner's Picture or Avatar]	**Age:** **Current Occupation:** **Education:** **Prior Work History:**

Provide a description about the learner, including any motivations, goals, and frustrations.

Learner Preparation

Technology Preferences

Challenges and Obstacles

Build Your Personal Learning Network

Use this job aid to help you build a personal learning network that supports your professional development.

Personal	Learning	Network
The *personal* element of these networks requires you to make connections and grow relationships with those who have different areas of expertise. As you collaborate, you exchange insights, answer questions, and discuss the goings-on in this new learning environment.	The *learning* element relates to staying on trend, and identifying and accessing key information. You'll swap ideas and expand upon what you learned on your own.	The *network* element defines the concept of a PLN. Within the network, you have an outlet for immediate outreach. You know who to turn to when a challenging or ambiguous concept arises, letting you focus on getting an answer, rather than worrying about where to start.

Create (and Refine) Your Personal Learning Network

- Set aside several hours to sort through those hundreds of emails and dozens of resources you wanted to look at "one day." Delete anything you've been holding on to for more than 30 days. There is too much information coming in for you to be concerned about what you have ignored for months already.
- Think about why you thought these resources were important at the time. Were they recommended by a trusted colleague? Did keywords stand out to you in the subject lines? Start to think about why you were collecting this content in the first place, but don't take the time now to read and try to learn. It's just too much.
- Create email rules that send these resources to a specific reading folder as they come in. And sort that folder by sender. Schedule one hour per week to review resources by sender. If you find you never read a content source, unsubscribe.
- Look through your list of recorded webinars and look for alternatives to watching one-hour recordings. Most webinar speakers have other, more accessible, microlearning resources like articles, blogs, and infographics. These shorter items will allow you to scan for relevance and decide if the longer webinar approach to the topic is worth your time.

Curate Your Content for Your Own Use

- When we consider curation for the learning field, we usually think about an expert commenting on content and sharing it with the field. But curation can, and should, start on a personal level.
- Once you have a list of content items that seem relevant, it's time to review them in depth and capturing notes on what makes those items important to your work and your personal development.
- If you can't capture even one note on why an item is important, discard it. It won't suddenly become important six months from now, because you won't remember it existed.
- To help organize information, use a free tool like Diigo to save and tag your online resources. For example, perhaps you've just read a great article on incorporating microlearning in a blended learning campaign. Enter the link into Diigo, add tags for microlearning, and include a few sentences about why this article was useful for you.
- As you collect more information on this topic, you will start to create a narrative about the topic, and identify content providers that resonate with you. And, when you have a need to create or discuss microlearning, for example, you will have trusted resources at hand.

Share Your Curated Insights

- Modern workplace learning is all about collaboration and sharing. You've started to connect all of the dots by collecting disparate content, organizing it, and providing thoughtful personal commentary on the value of the individual pieces.
- You can now make yourself part of someone else's PLN. Compile your curated insights and share them with your internal training team. Use social networks like Twitter, LinkedIn, or Facebook to share individual resources, summaries of topics, and your opinion on the value of content channels.

Additional Resources

Gottfredson, C., and B. Mosher. 2012. "Are You Meeting All Five Moments of Learning Need?" *Learning Solutions*, June 18. www.learningsolutionsmag.com /articles/949.

Hofmann, J. 2017. "The Learning Experience Architect: Reimagining Your Role." InSync Training blog, January 9. http://blog.insynctraining.com/6-learning -experience-architect-modern-learning.

Keegan, D. 2013. *Foundations of Distance Education*, 3rd Edition. New York: Routledge.

Love, S. 2016. "How to Conduct a Lightning Fast Needs Assessment Clients Will Love." ATD Insights blog, June 15. www.td.org/insights/how-to-conduct-a -lightning-fast-needs-assessment-clients-will-love.

Martin, N. 2014. "What Is Blended Learning, Really?" ATD Insights blog, June 24. www.td.org/insights/what-is-blended-learning-really.

Pappano, L. 2012. "The Year of the MOOC." *New York Times*, November 2. www.nytimes.com/2012/11/04/education/edlife/massive-open-online -courses-are-multiplying-at-a-rapid-pace.html.

Seitzinger, J. 2016. "You Just Might Be a Learning Experience Architect." LX Design blog, April 13. www.lxdesign.co/2016/04/you-just-might-be-a-learning -experience-architect.

Senffner, D., and L. Kepler. 2015. "Blended Learning That Works." *TD at Work*, October. Alexandria, VA: ATD Press.

Stober, D. 2015. "MOOCs Haven't Lived Up to the Hopes and the Hype, Stanford Participants Say." *Stanford News*, October 15. http://news.stanford.edu/2015 /10/15/moocs-no-panacea-101515.

Torrance, M. 2014. "Nine Moments of Learning." *TD*, September 8. www.td.org /magazines/td-magazine/nine-moments-of-learning.

2

Shaping the Future: Why Start a Blended Learning Program?

In This Chapter

- The shift from "push training" to "pull learning"
- The needs of modern learners
- How to manage the change to blended learning
- The partnership with the business and with learners

Thus chapter will address how blended learning meets the needs of modern learners while connecting with the business. It will discuss when, where, and how you can implement blended learning, and how you can prepare your organization to move from standalone delivery systems like e-learning or traditional classrooms to a more blended approach.

As you work your way through this book, you might realize that implementing blended learning is not exactly easy. When you begin to design a new blended learning campaign, you need to be aware of three things. First, blended learning is more than taking existing content and delivering it using various instructional technologies. It requires a strategic approach to instructional design and implementation, and a more detailed focus than traditionally delivered programs.

Second, the learning impact from blended learning is often not immediately realized. Depending on the instructional complexity of your design, a blended learning campaign could take weeks or months before it is formally concluded. And learners may not complete the campaign at the same time. So, you lose the opportunity, for example, to award completion certificates at the end of a two-day classroom program. This changes the business model of learning delivery.

And third, implementing blended learning can be expensive, especially when the approach is new to your organization. Investments need to be made in authoring tools, delivery technologies, and learning management systems. Additionally, the implementation team needs to be trained on how to effectively deploy these technologies, or you may need to go outside your organization to hire experts. Software licenses need to be maintained on an ongoing basis, and human resources need to be dedicated to the maintenance of learner records.

So, blended learning is more complicated to design, takes longer to roll out, and can be substantially more expensive than traditionally delivered content. If this is all true, why consider blended learning at all? Simply stated, it best meets the needs of today's learning environment.

Blended Learning in Today's Learning Environment

Twenty years ago, *learning environment* was not a phrase often used regarding corporate training. That's because almost all training was formally delivered to learners in a traditional classroom setting. Today, things are much different, and the learning environment has a strong influence on learning design.

Catherine Lombardozzi, author of *Learning Environments by Design* (2015), defines a learning environment as "a deliberately curated collection of materials and activities to support the development of a knowledge base or skill set. That curated collection can be made available in a variety of ways—from an email response one-on-one, to a web page available to anyone who needs it, to a dynamic online space that allows for both sharing and conversation."

This definition is a good start, which we will build on to further refine what is a modern learning environment and how blended learning fits in.

The Changing Workplace

The world of business and training is changing. When designing blended learning, you need to consider three driving factors—globalization, workforce mobility, and social collaboration—and recognize how they affect the learning environment. Traditional training methods limited the audience for training because the trainers and learners needed to be in the same place at the same time. New learning technologies allow us to reach a more diverse learner base, and changing business requirements mean we need to serve a globalized learner base. Because of this, talent development professionals need to recognize the influence that culture plays in the learning environment, especially those that have three or more cultures represented at the same time. Creating a true global learning environment takes planning, training, and understanding from all members of the implementation team. And it takes an understanding from the learners as well: This is new to all of us, and we can all learn from one another.

Worker mobility, and the technology that supports it, is now a critical success factor in most organizations. Whether employees are working on the road, traveling to a different office, logging in from home, or simply trying to get something done away from traditional workplace, the mobile workforce means you need to make sure content is where learners need to access it. In the rush to support this business need, the talent development function is not always strategic in determining what content should be mobilized and what delivery technologies are most appropriate.

Social collaboration is a required skill in this increasingly global and mobile world. Timely and collaborative social media platforms provide learners with the power to make sure that learning occurs during formal learning campaigns and continues afterward. Social collaborative tools can be used to build learning communities and continue the conversation started during the formal blended learning campaign.

Fortunately, by recognizing the trends toward globalization, mobility, and social collaboration, and by authentically designing programs that accommodate these trends, talent development professionals can do much more than just assist learners in mastering the content at hand. You can teach them how to be productive in the modern workplace.

From Push Training to Pull Learning

From an organizational perspective, things change slowly, and people are conditioned to do the same things the same way they've always done them. As we move from an industrial economy, which was revolutionary 100 years ago, to the new knowledge economy, we need to change how we're training. Interestingly, while we haven't yet changed the way we train, no other business function is still managed quite like it was a century ago. We know that classrooms and boot camps are not efficient, and people don't remember most of what they learn in those contexts, but we won't stop using them.

Learning is undergoing a vast rate of change due to the digital revolution. This revolution is forcing learning professionals to develop new models and change their approaches. Organizations are moving away from delivery-focused, instructor-centered events based on centralized and siloed content. Instead, they are moving toward ongoing, learner-centered, decentralized learning solutions that focus on results.

This evolution perfectly describes push training versus pull learning. Push training comes to the learners whether they're ready (and willing) or not. In comparison, pull learning is made available to learners when they need it. This is a major change in culture that most companies do not know how to manage. As partners in the business, talent development professionals need to prove the value of including more pull learning opportunities.

To meet the needs of modern learners, you need to focus on the pull learning model as a significant part of your blend, where people can connect and learn from one another. Based on this, we can expand on Catherine Lombardozzi's definition of the learning environment. If you recognize that you are moving from a push training culture to a pull learning culture, the learning environment can be, at least in part, strongly influenced by the needs of the modern workplace and of the modern learner.

The Needs of Modern Learners

Many resources attempt to describe the characteristics of modern learners, and there is a lot of commonality in what you will find. Modern learners are always looking to learn more. They are not satisfied with just knowing the what; they also want to know the why and the what's next. In this vein, modern learners often design their own personal learning paths.

It can be difficult for even the most dedicated learner to stay engaged in a multi-week or multi-month learning campaign of different instructional technologies and self-directed work. How do you keep up the momentum? You can start by applying adult learning principles.

While some of the characteristics of modern learners have changed, the basic tenants of adult learning principles still apply. Blended learning campaigns provide vast opportunities to incorporate the tenets of adult learning theory. Let's review adult learning principles and explore a few ways to ensure they are addressed in your blended learning designs (Figure 2-1).

Figure 2-1. Characteristics of Adult Learners

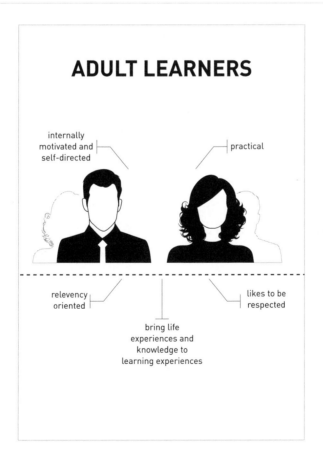

Adults Are Internally Motivated and Self-Directed

Let's face it: Most people want to do a good job, and when your learners *must* obtain a new skill to be successful at their job, they will do what they have to do to learn that skill. If formal training is unavailable, they will find another way to get information, including accessing help facilities, asking colleagues, and relying on search engines.

Consider that many modern learners rely on social networks, whether in person or online, to get answers and share knowledge. (Jane Hart's Learning in the Workplace Survey identified knowledge sharing within one's team to be the most useful way to learn in the workplace.) Modern learners capitalize on the knowledge and experience of their co-workers to get things done, including in everyday conversations and meetings. If someone on their team doesn't have the answer, they often turn to personal and professional networks, search engines, blogs, or newsfeeds. They strongly prefer these options over traditional learning and e-learning.

RESOURCE

Check out the results of Jane Hart's "Learning in the Workplace Survey" to see how more than 5,000 professionals worldwide rated the value of 10 different ways of learning in the workplace (http://c4lpt.co.uk/litw-results).

You can take advantage of this motivation in blended learning campaigns by providing a formal tool set learners can access as needed. For example, communities of learning and e-learning tutorials that address basic skills, followed up with virtual lessons for those who might need more practice, are a great way to allow motivated learners manage their own learning.

Self-directed learning may not always address every moment of learning need; this is especially true when people are learning complex new tasks or practicing new skills or behaviors. Learners need to understand what they need to know and what resources are available to them to meet their goals. You can build upon this internal motivation, instead of stopping at making content available without guidance on how it should be used.

Adults Bring Life Experiences and Knowledge to the Learning Environment

Whenever you bring learners together in real time, be sure to include ample opportunities for them to interact and collaborate. Minimize lecture during live sessions, and allow learners to build upon existing knowledge and experiences.

For example, when using a virtual classroom to deliver a lesson, avoid the one-hour webinar. Listening to a lecture for 45 minutes and asking questions at the end does not support the way adults learn best. Even the most motivated and self-directed learners will find it difficult to remain engaged when they are not actively part of the process. Instead, the design should anticipate learner interaction every three to five minutes, and lectures should be kept to less than five minutes.

Adults Are Relevancy Oriented; Every Lesson and Activity Needs an Outcome

This is especially important in any type of online environment because it is easy to lose your learners' attention. The fact is, online learners have little tolerance for content they perceive to be "nice to know." If there is a topic or activity that doesn't resonate in a traditional setting, they need to sit through it and be polite. However, when that training is online and people are learning at their desks, they will have other priorities calling for their attention, so facilitators need to work harder to keep learners engaged. Remember, modern learners are overworked, overwhelmed, and distracted (Tauber and Johnson 2014). This means learning needs to be easy, focused, and supported.

The design of a blended learning program should constantly answer the question, "Why is this important to me?" Just because a new initiative is important to the organization does not mean the initiative's relevance is immediately apparent to the learner. Ultimately, the learners are the arbiter of what's important to them. Blended learning makes it easy for learners to make decisions about when to engage or disengage. It's your job to ensure that adult learners are motivated to participate. Case-based learning, problem-based learning, and hands-on application practice are instructional strategies that drive home relevance.

Keep all blended learning lessons—whether self-directed or live—focused and action oriented. Every activity must have a point that is obvious to the learner, and each activity should be debriefed or summarized to reinforce that point. Assessments and tests can help with this reinforcement. The key is to make sure every moment spent learning is perceived as a good investment of time by the learner.

And be prepared: Some learners participating in a blended learning design will decide that a piece of content is not relevant. If they make that decision, they often will opt out of some lessons. Blended learning doesn't only provide flexibility to content delivery; it provides flexibility for learners to make decisions about what is relevant to them. This can be uncomfortable for those who design training. Blended learning forces you to give up control of the learning process and be more concerned with learning outcomes.

Adults Are Practical

While theory can provide background, adult learners want opportunities to practice so they can be confident about being able to perform a new skill back in the workplace. This is an area talent development professionals still need to master; we know how to push content through e-learning lessons and webinar-type lectures, but we have minimized—if not eliminated—opportunities to practice skills. And we're missing out on some fabulous opportunities: instructional technologies such as maker spaces and virtual classrooms provide great ways to practice. Imagine a customer service representative role-playing through application sharing in a virtual classroom. This is even more realistic than an equivalent role-play in a face-to-face environment, because the customer service agent will be using this skill while on the telephone. Why bring people face-to-face to teach them skills they will never use in a face-to-face environment? It isn't authentic.

Practicality also means making sure learning is available at the right place when the moment of learning need arises. Workers travel between home offices and traditional office buildings, they work from coffeehouses and airports, and they expect to be able to learn wherever they happen to be. As far as what device they use, it comes down to learner choice. People are more comfortable with personal devices they already know how to navigate. For instance, a left-handed person might have the computer mouse on the opposite side of a keyboard from a right-handed person. Switching computers for a day could lead to frustration for both.

Adult Learners Want Respect

Instead of focusing on what learners don't know, facilitators of blended learning need to focus on what learners *do* know. You need to lose the sage on the stage mentality and create a more collaborative rapport. Online learners need to be more than a name in a learning management system—they should be treated as colleagues. You should strive to recall stories and experiences that learners have shared and bring these into future conversations.

It's easy to lecture in an online learning environment, but long-winded lectures that have not been designed to help learners meet their individual goals do not show respect for the learners. Conversations, meaningful activities, and thoughtful design do.

PRO TIP

It's important to keep in mind the generational differences among learners, but remember there are more similarities than what we're conventionally told. I once facilitated a group of talent development professionals trying to create a strategy to engage young learners just joining their workforce. (This was at a traditional financial institution.) After 30 minutes of brainstorming and designing a strategy to engage Millennials in their learning initiatives, they realized that the same strategies would also engage the older workforce. The difference—the only difference—was that people with a more traditional learning background didn't demand as much from the learning function.

How Has the Current Learning Landscape Changed?

Now we can expand the definition of learning environment even more. The learning environment is composed not just of the characteristics of the workforce and the learner; it also includes where and when learning needs to occur.

Where People Learn

When planning a blend, the question "Where will learning happen?" is critical to selecting appropriate learning environments. In the digital age, it's important to note that learning environments are "places" rather than technologies. We can deploy virtual classroom platforms or e-learning modules in multiple learning environments, including the traditional classroom.

Identifying where learning takes place involves the ability to deploy instructional technologies or methods within a physical or virtual space. For clarity, let's look at four places where learning can take place:

- **In the classroom.** Traditional, face-to-face learning environments include a number of defining characteristics, such as physical space, learner co-location, and the instructor. This is the place our organizations automatically think of when they ask for training; it's the most easily recognized. We can incorporate instructional technologies, lectures, printed participant guides, and other learning assets to support an in-class learning experience.

- **On a computer.** Thanks to virtualization, desktop or laptop computers have evolved into important places of learning. My definition assumes two things: The computers are not in a classroom, and learners are physically separated from one another. If those two assumptions are not met, the computer doesn't act as a place of learning, and instead becomes an instructional technology.

- **On a mobile device.** It sounds counterintuitive, but mobile devices are a place of learning. We can implement e-learning, video, and even virtual classrooms on mobile devices. Smartphones and tablets provide our learners with the freedom to learn wherever they are, whenever they have a moment of need. Please note that laptop computers, while portable, don't qualify as a mobile device because their functionality matches that of desktop computers.

- **On the job (OTJ).** If your learners are performing a job and learning a new skill at the same time, the place of learning is OTJ. This can include formal mentoring arrangements or informal learning in a moment of need. Regardless of the technologies leveraged, including computers and mobile devices, if learning is taking place in the field, the *where* remains on the job.

When selecting a place of learning, consider context. Ask, "Is this the place where learners will use that skill in the real world?" For example, teaching a medical device sales person how to use a new ordering system on the tablet they take to client meetings provides a more authentic learning experience than teaching that skill in the classroom through a lecture. Ultimately, blended learning provides us with the latitude to match learning objectives to the most appropriate treatments. If we support how learners work with where they will learn, the blend becomes more robust.

PRO TIP

Learning authenticity means that the learning presents content to participants in a way that mirrors how those skills will be used. The modern workplace learning environment is about creating experiences that are very relatable and accessible. To create an authentic learning experience, learning professionals must make sure that we are delivering content to learners in the right place.

When People Learn

When designing learning campaigns, you also need to consider *when* learning will take place. Is the experience formal (scheduled, measurable, and structured) or on-demand (just in time and less structured)? Do participants need to learn something while actively in the task and doing the work, or do they need a more formal, structured foundation before attempting the task in a real work environment?

After considering where people learn, answering the question of "when" is easy. A classroom is a formal event that is pre-scheduled and definitely outside the workplace. The time spent learning in a classroom is managed and measurable.

A great model for identifying when people need to learn is the Five Moments of Learning Need, as identified by Conrad Gottfredson and Bob Mosher. Learning professionals need to create learning that supports five different moments of need:

- when learning something new
- when learning more
- when applying what they have learned
- when solving problems
- when things change.

When designing any piece of a blended learning campaign, you need to think about which moments of need it can support. Whenever possible, it's optimal that a learning resource—like an e-learning program, video, infographic, or job aid—support multiple moments of need. For example, a job aid could be used to teach a new process through a virtual classroom (learning something new) and on the job (when applying what they have learned).

If you consider the five moments of learning need, in-person classroom training generally addresses the first moment of need: when learning something new. It can also address the last moment of need: when things change. What in-person classroom training cannot do is support a learner who is applying what they learned on the job or when things go wrong.

When learning occurs at the desktop or on a mobile device, it can be either formal (for example, scheduled virtual classrooms) or on-demand (for example, e-learning or video). When designed authentically and thoughtfully, desktop learning and mobile learning can support every moment of learning need.

OTJ is a less formal and more on-demand experience. For example, to learn how to create a new PowerPoint template for a deliverable later in the same week, a learner may choose to seek guidance from a colleague, access an online tutorial, or review an online forum. This less formal type of OTJ training is often called *just in time* (JIT), meaning it is accessed at the moment of need and applies what was learned.

Managing the Change to Blended Learning

As organizations adopt different instructional technologies, the natural inclination is to focus on making the technology work. It needs to work across the network, it needs to be secure, and it needs to be accessible to your learners. The problem is, organizations are often so focused on technology that they forget that transitioning from traditional learning environments to blended learning environments is a change issue. After all, if the technology doesn't work, they can find something to replace it. Adopting and excelling at blended learning designs is much more about attitudinal change than it is about implementing technology. Ultimately, people need to believe that the virtual classroom will work. However, organizations spend more time worrying about firewalls, security, hardware, and software (all important topics) than they do thinking about adoption and usability.

If the transition to blended learning fails, it can be hard to recover. Learners and other stakeholders will be quick to assume that blended learning doesn't work for their topic, for their audience, or for them as individuals. Therefore, it is critical that you consider the transition to blended learning campaigns as a change management initiative.

The Change Curve

Each organization has its champions committed to blended learning success. Implementation teams, those responsible for the creation and deployment of the blend, must anticipate that members of their target audience will experience and react to the transition differently. Understanding the change curve helps us plan accordingly. The four stages of the change curve are denial, resistance, exploration, and commitment. Let's examine these stages so you can recognize where your organization's blended learning adoption falls on the change curve, and how to help move to the next stage.

Denial

Any learning implementation faces the denial stage. At this point, individuals may appear complacent about the change, expressing neither support nor disproval for the new initiative. By most appearances, they look like team players. But in practice, they cling to the comfort of traditional processes and methods.

My professional advice? At the beginning of any blended learning implementation, assume that you have team members in denial. You can identify them by the language they use to discuss the program. For example, if you hear someone say, "This is just a passing fad," or "The traditional environment worked so well, I doubt blended learning can replace it," they're likely in denial.

Combat denial by encouraging participation in new blended learning opportunities. Shore skill-building exercises and leverage volunteers early on. Volunteers who opt in to programs willingly, and participate in practical, relevant learning experiences often become the program champions down the road. Furthermore, their feedback often proves more constructive and helpful than resistant learners forced to participate in a program they don't believe in.

Resistance

Resistance may be futile, but it's a very common stage of blended learning implementation. At the point when learners—and maybe even stakeholders—realize that blended learning is actually going to replace their tried-and-true traditional training, you'll hear:

- "My content won't work in a blended format. I have to teach it in a classroom setting."
- "We all know technology doesn't improve training! I've been in tech-heavy programs and I didn't learn a single useful skill."
- "Face-to-face instruction is the only way the organizational message can be effectively communicated."

Under the anger and obstinance lies the true concern: that the content, work, and methodology people have spent years developing won't exist down the road. Empathize with these concerns, and remind yourself that you can't force people to accept change, no matter how well-designed and potentially effective the new model.

Instead, respond to their questions with factual answers. Use data and theory to address concerns, not unsubstantiated projections. Make training and blended learning experiences available, so people can discover their power on their own. And always, always include ways for your team to share feedback, both positive and negative, about the new learning process. By including the team and your learners in the process, you'll empower them to work through their resistance to change.

Exploration

When learners begin to participate in the blended learning process, the exploration stage of the change curve begins. During this phase, the conversations become more positive (although often noncommittal), and pointed questions will arise. You'll likely hear:

- "I'm going to try out that one new learning program, but I can't promise I'll like it."
- "If the program doesn't succeed, who will be held responsible?"
- "How do we know if our learners are gaining the necessary skills?"

Latch on to any sign of enthusiasm! Build on this slight progress to create momentum around the blend, this will help carry you toward the final stage of the change curve.

Commitment

We strive to achieve the commitment stage for blended learning. At this point, people expect blended learning, and understand their roles in the (now commonplace) practice. Teams accept that this approach provides an alternative option to traditional training, and they can leverage it when it provides an improved solution to a need.

Team members will reach the commitment stage at their own pace. You can gauge whether there's a commitment consensus when you hear statements like:

- "This process can be more effective than the way we used to teach this content."
- "Let's brainstorm with the instructional team to find a way to make this module even better for our learners."
- "I have a new project coming up. Can I use this same blended learning approach for that initiative, too?"

Katrina Baker, author of *Corporate Training Tips & Tricks* (2017), offers insights to help move organizations along the blended learning change curve. Her blog post "Virtual Classroom Adoption: The 4 Stages of Change" outlines a few of the key takeaways for managing new learning implementations. I use these takeaways to guide my work, and you may find them helpful, too:

- **Start small.** If key stakeholders at the top resist the change, start with a small group of learners to demonstrate the capabilities of your new idea.
- **Prepare for pushback.** It may feel like a natural progression for those of us in learning and development, but this constitutes a major change in the status quo. Resistance to change from learners, stakeholders, and even your fellow learning professionals is natural, and it often presents itself through fear.
- **Be willing to edit.** New initiatives are amorphous. Don't marry yourself to the details. Instead, gather feedback from learners during the pilot and make changes as you go. Work with the mantra, "Add. Delete. Refine."

- **Celebrate successes of all sizes.** Change management provides a serious organizational challenge. It feels exhausting and exhilarating and overwhelming. When things go right, acknowledge it. When things go wrong, openly discuss and work through it.

We have to remember that the change curve isn't a one-and-done cycle. It's an iterative process that repeats itself. Keep an eye out for regression and perpetually support advancement toward commitment.

TOOL

Use the "Plotting the Change Curve" tool at the end of this chapter to plot where your organization is on the change curve when considering blended approaches to instructional design, instructional technologies, delivery approaches, and informal learning.

A Modern Workplace Learning Mindset

Many experts in social and informal learning encourage learning professionals to focus on embedding learning in the workflow, instead of focusing on creating a portfolio of e-learning, classroom training, and PowerPoint slides. That's not to say that formal training has no part in modern blended learning design. It does. But it's part of the blend; not the focus.

According to Jane Hart of the Centre for Modern Workplace Learning, to best serve modern learners and the modern workplace, you need to adopt a modern workplace learning mindset.

This means embracing that learning happens without you—informally while people are working, not through formal channels. This type of learning comes from interacting with peers and just doing one's job. And it's just as important as learning that is created by your team. This mindset supports a much wider range of learning experiences.

You also need to encourage learners to pursue this independent type of learning, and encourage them to find answers and create their own personal learning paths. This means letting go of the control of learning.

Remember, your team is not solely responsible for all learning. Managers and learners have a responsibility to ensure learning happens, and your role is to support that learning no matter how it occurs. This encourages a new partnership between L&D and the business.

Strategically adopting a modern workplace learning mindset can help you move your organization through the change curve. Supporting informal learning is critical, and your role is more about supporting learning outcomes and delivering content. If you can do that, blended learning will be valued by learners as a flexible approach that fits their learning requirements while supporting business goals.

Chapter 3 will discuss how you can design your formal blended learning campaigns so they continue to be useful, even after they end. In effect, it will discuss how you accomplish embedding learning in the workflow.

Increasing Acceptance—Start With New Hire Training

You have identified where your organization is on the change curve regarding the adoption of blended learning. And, you are working with L&D to adopt a modern workplace learning mindset. The final piece of your change management strategy is to encourage learners to accept blended learning as a preferred way to learn, and to fully participate in the experience. How do you get that done?

Selecting the right program with which to introduce the approach to your corporate learners is just as important as designing blended learning campaigns correctly. New hire training is the perfect place to start. Introducing blended learning during new hire orientation increases adoption, accelerates learning for the new hires, and is authentic.

Because this is the first experience new employees have with your organization's learning function, you're sending a clear message that blended learning is considered a legitimate way to teach and learn. In addition, you'll be establishing a more authentic learning environment because they will be learning at their own desks, near their own co-workers, and using the technology they will use to do their jobs.

After your blended learning new hire orientation has been around for several years, there will be fewer and fewer naysayers. The most vocal employees will have experienced and bought into blended learning.

Here are some example elements you can include in a virtual new hire orientation that takes advantage of the positive energy your new hires have:

- Focus on what they're excited about. What's their job? What should they expect day-to-day? How will they learn to be a valuable part of your team?

- Have them meet their supervisor and their co-workers, and get the lay of the land. Most learning takes place informally while doing one's job, so include that experience early in their career so collaboration becomes the norm.

- Schedule regular, maybe even daily, lessons to complete throughout the entire new hire curriculum. Discuss details like benefits 30 days in, when new employees are much closer to needing to decide about them. Provide a self-paced tutorial on the history of the company, instead of lecturing about something that's not immediately relevant to people's jobs. HR topics can be sprinkled over the course of the first week or two, allowing learners to not just master the information, but integrate that into their workflow.

- Use a blended learning campaign to teach smaller tasks, and then encourage new employees to practice what they learn. Start each day with a live, one-hour session dedicated to teaching the basics of a skill and providing resources they can use to practice it. Then give them tasks related to those lessons to complete during the day. These tasks might include interviewing supervisors, co-workers, and potential clients; taking their first customer service phone call; or creating a spreadsheet for the finance department. Finally, organize another live, one-hour session where new hires can debrief their successes and be coached on how to do tasks better the next day.

By designing a campaign that allows your new hires to integrate into their teams, practice new skills, and still ask for help in a safe environment, you can have a very positive influence on your workplace culture moving forward.

PRO TIP

Blended learning campaigns eliminate the "drinking from the fire hose" sensation of new employee training, and allow you to present the most relevant information at the most appropriate times. I still remember being 21 years old and learning about my health insurance options during my second hour on the job; I wasn't even eligible for insurance for 60 days! Even after many years, I can recall how overwhelmed I felt by that process. Blended learning can help.

Partnering With the Business

In some organizations, training initiatives can feel like an afterthought. When a business initiative is identified, developed, and rolled out, training gets involved very late in the process. The business tells you what it thinks the training need is, and then you must rush to fill that need with limited resources, budget, and time.

These limitations don't allow you to design the best solutions. This role of order taker doesn't use your expertise, and certainly doesn't allow you to be a full partner in the success of the business. As the learning landscape becomes more learner directed, and blended learning campaigns are more widespread, your relationship with the business needs to change. Needs analysis has to take place much earlier and must be more strategic.

Creating a stronger partnership with the business means that you need to more strongly connect business goals with learning outcomes. Here are some guidelines for developing this partnership:

- **Reinforce the modern workplace learning mindset.** When suggesting a blended learning approach to a business sponsor, share more than the tools you're going to use. Explain that much of the learning will be directed by the individual learners at their desks, on their mobile devices, and on the job. You will support those efforts by ensuring that the right resources are in the right place when the learners need them. Don't just share the "what" of your design; also share the "why." Share case studies, anecdotes, and literature that support your approach. If you are well prepared, the other stakeholders will be more confident in your suggestions.

- **Change the perception of your role.** You want to go from being seen as an order taker and event manager to a performance consultant. Your job should not be to implement presupposed solutions; rather it's to identify the best solution for the problem. Sometimes, that will be a formal training initiative. Sometimes, it will be performance support embedded in the workflow. You are no longer supporting training; you are supporting learning. You need to be included in new business initiatives early on, so you can identify potential performance gaps and plan to close those gaps in the most economical and nonintrusive way possible.

- **Explain that mastery of a new task or skill takes time.** It does not occur during a 30-minute e-learning course or a two-day workshop. Rather, to achieve mastery, learning needs to be continuous. To support this goal of perpetual learning, your blended learning campaign needs to "time release" content. However, this can be frustrating to the business because it takes a long time to complete. Acknowledge this up front.

- **Show that blended learning is more than a way to save money.** It is true that blended learning can save money in terms of travel, classrooms, and related costs, but it's important that the business understands that blended learning is not about saving money. In fact, you may not even save money in the beginning (although eventually, it can certainly result in a huge cost savings). As a good partner, you should provide a true budget, and an explanation about why the costs might be higher than may have been expected. Remind them that the goal is improved performance results and learning outcomes, and that the investments made now can be shared among multiple initiatives.

- **Learning is a shared responsibility.** Managers can't simply turn over their employees to be trained; they need to help learners make decisions about where to focus their limited learning time. And then they need to support those decisions. As managers see their employees gaining and mastering more skills, they are more likely to get involved in the evaluation process, perhaps completing observation forms and updating the LMS.

By partnering with the business, you can increase engagement in blended learning. If this happens, engagement in work should also increase, as well as the quality of job performance. This strongly connects the business with the learning function.

Partnering With Learners

Creating blended learning that only addresses when your audiences need to learn something new, while ignoring other moments of learning need like when things go wrong or when applying what's been learned, reinforces the old paradigm. This comes at the expense of knowledge sharing, search engines, conversations with peers, and professional networks.

Julie Dirksen, author of *Design for How People Learn,* suggests that learning professionals tend to overlook the contributions learners can make to the partnership. To encourage collaboration, she recommends including learners in the evaluation process, encouraging them to "work out loud," and including user-generated content in the design. In her blog post "Partner With Your Learners," Julie provides a framework for becoming advocates for modern learning:

- **Evaluate.** Modern blended learning equips learners to take control of their own learning pathways. If we build in moments of self-evaluation, learners more easily connect the learning program to their personal performance. When appropriate, encourage learners to review and evaluate one another's progress. By engaging them in the evaluation process, learners commit to the program more willingly and assume personal responsibility for their own skill building.

- **Work out loud.** *Show Your Work* author Jane Bozarth demonstrates the enormous value of having people make their work visible to others. Encourage learners to ask questions. Provide spaces where examples of learner work products can be shared. By discussing and sharing with others, learners solidify their skills, turning knowledge into true performance improvement.

- **Collaborate to create.** Social collaboration constitutes a key piece of any blend. Expand upon basic forums and inter-learner discussion by inviting your audience to join the content creation process. Incorporate learner experience documentation into the program. Use the information and lessons learned for future program offerings. Record questions about existing content and use them as a basis for conversations with subject matter experts. The possibilities for collaboration are endless, and so are the potential rewards.

By partnering with learners to determine when they want and need to learn, you create a culture that encourages learners to use the resources you provide. Develop a partnership with your learners by teaching them how to address the individual moments of need using resources from the formal program, and give them permission to use these resources later. It helps if you provide typical situations of when they might use these resources, for example:

- When a customer is irate, use this infographic to help manage the conversation. Hang it by your desk so it is available when you need it.

- You probably won't need to create a pivot table right away. Instead of memorizing the steps, let's explore what the help facility can do to walk you through the process.

Make sure learners know how to access resources. It's not enough to have the content in the right spot—you need to teach them how to access and use the tools in their moment of need. The more you can take all those microlearning elements and make them part of macro-learning, the more reusable the tools become. Blended learning materials aren't meant to sit on a shelf and never get used again.

Convincing learners that the resources you provide are valuable will be the most difficult part of the change. How can you train them so their first instinct is to access your learning resources in a moment of need? Why would they go to your resources instead of calling over their cubicle or not learning at all? How do you get them to participate in this new learning environment?

PRO TIP

Katrina Baker leaves us with this thought: "When learners trust you, they become more willing to try new things. If you consistently bring them tools they can use, they will in turn give you the space to be creative. Ask what they need, then bring them some interesting options—maybe an e-learning course, or a document and some short videos. Ask the learners what they think. Ask for the good and bad. Revise your materials, and incorporate the feedback into your next project."

We must acknowledge the fact that learners are out there getting content on their own. Your job in this new modern learning culture is to make sure they have the tools they need to do their jobs, that the content is correct, and that it's easy to use. The content needs to be engaging, relevant, and accessible. It needs to be right on target.

What's Next

We've spent a lot of time discussing how the learning environment has changed, and how you can support that change, including becoming a true partner to your learners and with the business. The discussion has been at a very high level, but it's time to dig into the details of building and implementing a blended learning campaign.

Chapter 3 will focus on designing the formal and informal components of the learning campaign, and connecting the dots between resources. Special focus will be given to extending the learning past the formal event, and how to facilitate the experience.

Questions to Explore

- If you have implemented blended learning in your organization before, what surprised you about the design, cost, and instructional complexity? How did these factors influence the quality and success of the campaign?

- Globalization, mobilization, and social collaborative technologies are major business drivers. How are they affecting your learning design?
- Are you designing learning resources for formal programs that are meant to be used when learners are doing the job? How do you communicate the dual use?
- Has your organization experienced a blended learning fail? What was the cause? What have you changed to mitigate the problem in the future?

Tools for Support

Plotting the Change Curve

Use this worksheet to plot where your organization is on the change curve when considering blended approaches to instructional design, instructional technologies, delivery approaches, and informal learning. Shade in the quadrant that best describes where your organization is in each category.

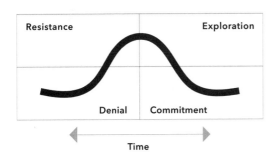

Instructional Design Approaches

_____

_____

_____

_____

_____

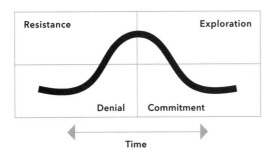

Instructional Technology Adoption

_____

_____

_____

_____

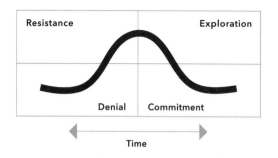

Delivery Approaches

_____

_____

_____

_____

_____

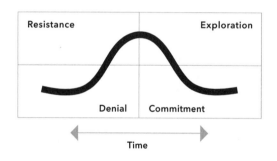

Informal and Organic Learning

_____

_____

_____

_____

_____

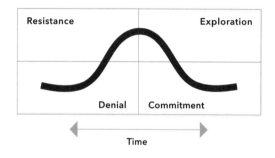

Budgeting the Time, Place,
and Space

_____

_____

_____

_____

_____

Additional Resources

Babcock, B. 2012. "Dealing With Redundancy." Grafton Haymes blog, March 27. www.graftonhaymes.co.uk/2012/03/27/dealing-with-redundancy-by-barbara -babcock.

Dirksen, J. 2016. *Design for How People Learn,* 2nd Edition. San Francisco: Peachpit.

Gottfredson, C., and B. Mosher. 2012. "Are You Meeting All Five Moments of Learning Need?" *Learning Solutions,* June 18. www.learningsolutionsmag.com /articles/949.

Hofmann, J. 2016. *Engaging Modern Learners: When to Push and When to Pull.* Portsmouth, NH: InSync Training.

Knowles, M.S., E.F. Holton III, and R.A. Swanson. 2011. *The Adult Learner: The Definitive Classic in Adult Education and Human Resource Development,* 7th Edition. New York: Routledge.

Lombardozi, C. 2015. *Learning Environments by Design.* Alexandria, VA: ATD Press.

Seitzinger, J. 2016. "You Just Might Be a Learning Experience Architect." LX Design blog, April 13. www.lxdesign.co/2016/04/you-just-might-be-a-learning-experience -architect.

Tauber, T., and D. Johnson. 2014. "Meet the Modern Learner (Infographic)." Bersin by Deloitte. www.bersin.com/Practice/Detail.aspx?id=18071.

Thakur, S. 2010. "Stages of the Change Curve." Bright Hub Project Management blog, September 18. www.brighthubpm.com/change-management/87472-stages-of-the -change-curve.

3

Designing Your Blended Learning Program: How Do You Start?

In This Chapter

- The importance of the needs assessment
- The design process for the blended learning campaign
- Instructional strategies, techniques, and technologies
- A course map to manage instructional complexity

You've probably heard the phrase, "There's never time to do it right, but always time to do it over." This is simply not true when it comes to implementing a blended learning design.

For example, it's common to assume that anything that can be taught in a face-to-face environment can also be taught in a virtual classroom. Trainers bring existing presentation slides into the virtual environment and deliver them without any planning or design because they assume the transition will be easy. Only after a less than optimal delivery does the implementation team realize that content needs to be redesigned to be optimized for the environment.

When delivering a face-to-face program for the first time, it's usually immediately obvious what design elements are working and not working. And it can be relatively easy to fix problems before the next delivery—you can tighten the script, clarify activity instructions, adjust slides, and edit handouts. Skilled facilitators can even adjust the design in the moment if it becomes obvious the learner's needs aren't being met.

Not so with blended learning.

Consider this relatively simple one-week-long blended learning design, consisting of two live online lessons, one e-learning lesson, and one self-directed activity (Figure 3-1). There are a variety of ways for this blended design to fail, and only one way for it to be successful.

Figure 3-1. Sample Weeklong Blended Learning Design

The blend will be successful if learners attend the live lessons, complete the self-directed lesson, and perceive value in completing the self-directed activity. If all this occurs, you can be reasonably sure that the role-play assessment will allow the learners to achieve the desired performance outcome. However, this blended learning program can fail for a variety of reasons; for example:

- **Learners do not value the self-directed lessons and activities.**
  If there is a face-to-face element to a training program, many learners will assume that the important knowledge and skills will be conveyed during that event, and the pre-work and other self-directed assignments are optional.

Facilitators often reinforce this behavior by incorporating the knowledge that was supposed to be learned in a self-directed format into the live class. If the learners do not do the self-directed work, but still meet the learning objectives, the design has still failed. This simply means the self-directed work was not required to meet the learning goals.

- **Technology does not work.** There are multiple places in this blended learning design were technology could fail for an individual learner or the entire cohort. Even one technology roadblock can become a detour for learners who are already overscheduled, overworked, and overwhelmed. For example, if learners cannot download a video because they do not have the proper credentials, they may put off troubleshooting the issue past the point where they are inclined to participate.

- **Instructions are not clear.** In a traditional learning environment, the facilitator can usually determine when learners are not able to complete an activity or move on to the next content block. In a blended learning environment, facilitators don't always have that immediate feedback. When instructions about how to complete self-directed activities, how to participate in a virtual breakout, or even how to fully participate to get credit are not clear, modern learners may decide their time is better spent on projects where they can see positive results.

These are just a few of the problems you may encounter when implementing a blend, and there are certainly many more. Fortunately, it can be relatively painless if you put the time in up front to create a strong implementation plan that addresses the needs of the business, utilizes strong instructional design, and incorporates a content strategy plan. Do this before you develop content, and you will have a blueprint to direct your implementation team.

This chapter focuses on how to successfully implement the entire blended learning campaign. Your goal is to create an experience that extends the learning beyond the formal element, and ensures your learners' needs are being met while supporting business requirements.

As the learning experience architect, you are responsible for the blended learning program's design and implementation, which includes an up-front needs analysis, instructional design, content strategy, technology selection, pilot and evaluation strategy, and change management needs. This project management role is critical in the modern learning landscape. Without someone managing all the parts, blended learning implementation has a high risk of failure. You don't need to author all the content or facilitate the learning experience, but you do need to understand enough about each part of the process to create and manage a comprehensive plan. The design and implementation steps are:

1. Conduct the needs assessment.
2. Design the blended learning campaign.
3. Create the project proposal.
4. Design and implement the content strategy.
5. Manage the facilitation plan.

This chapter will address the first two steps, and provide a series of tools to help you along the way. Chapter 4 touches on the last three, and chapter 5 covers developing the evaluation plan to assess the success or failure of your blended learning program.

Conduct the Needs Assessment

A successful blended learning campaign meets the needs of the business. As organizations become more global, virtual, and mobile, their learning requirements become more complex, and the learning that supports the business must evolve to meet those requirements. A strong focus on business requirements and organizational readiness encourages the adoption of a modern workplace learning mindset, and strengthens the partnership between talent development and the business.

Before you start the design process, you need a comprehensive understanding of the business requirements. Especially important to blended learning design are linking learning outcomes to business requirements and determining organizational readiness.

Linking Learning Outcomes to Business Requirements

When designing a blended learning solution, a critical part of the process will be to link the learning outcomes to business requirements. This should always be a part of the needs analysis process. Depending on the instructional complexity of the blend, its development can be expensive, and the implementation timeline could take many months. If you go through this potentially expensive and time-consuming process without being certain you are meeting the business need, you might be delivering content that's not needed.

Brandon Hall Group's *State of Learning & Development 2016: Ready to Evolve* study cites aligning learning strategy with the business as the most important initiative for learning professionals. The study also identifies the five learning outcomes that are most critical to the business:

- improved organizational performance
- improved individual performance
- improved employee engagement
- reduced skill or competency gaps
- reduced time to productivity.

Being conversant in these learning outcomes and how blended learning can support them will help you manage initial conversations with your clients and ensure your design is meeting business requirements. As you become more adept at designing and implementing blended learning campaigns, you'll be able to supplement your ideas with data specific to your organization.

As you explore the need for a blended learning campaign, you'll document needs specific to your client. In addition to these client-specific needs, be sure to ask how the desired learning solution can meet the business outcome. It may be difficult for your client to articulate the business need for a perceived training requirement, because the need feels obvious. To help a client prepare, share the business requirements worksheet prior to the design kickoff meeting, and give context around why the information is critical to the project.

TOOL

The "Business Requirements" tool at the end of this chapter will help you demonstrate why linking learning outcomes to business needs is critical to the project.

Determining Organizational Readiness

Chapter 2 examined where your organization might be on the change curve regarding blended learning. No matter where your organization is—whether it's denial, resistance, exploration, or commitment—you need to determine if it's ready to adopt blended learning campaigns as a learning norm.

When evaluating organizational readiness, you should consider the learning culture, organizational support, technology tools and infrastructure, training team readiness, and learner readiness. Does your organization have a culture that values learning? Is your organization actively engaged in moving through the change curve? Is there a methodology in place for piloting new instructional technologies? Does your training team have the skills they need to be successful? Do learners have access to the appropriate devices and equipment to fully participate?

TOOL

To determine your organizational readiness, use the "Blended Learning Organizational Readiness Assessment" tool at the end of this chapter.

The better you know your learner, the better your blended learning program will be. Use the learning persona worksheet introduced in chapter 1 to ensure you understand your target audience, and how ready it is for blended learning.

If blended learning is new to your organization, you probably won't score as high on the organizational readiness assessment as more mature learning organizations. That doesn't mean you cannot or should not implement blended learning; however, it does mean you might want to start with a less complex learning design and pilot the design with individuals open to providing constructive feedback about the process. Any components that you indicate as "not yet prepared" pose a potential risk, and you should discuss them with your client and with the implementation team. Document your opinions and your discussions, and then find ways to evolve your organization's readiness as part of the process.

This is an exercise you should conduct at the beginning of every blended learning initiative, because organizational readiness might be different from department to department in your organization.

Design the Blended Learning Campaign

Instructional design is always critical to the success of any formal learning program. That said, as you become more familiar with a format, especially face-to-face delivery, it's important not to shortcut the design process even if you have formulas that work. There are several popular instructional design models; the ADDIE model may be the most common. The five phases in this model are analysis, design, development, implementation, and evaluation.

The design phase is when you create the blueprint for an entire training program by identifying or validating learning objectives. For blended learning, the design phase produces:

- tasks the learners will be able to perform at the end of the campaign, represented as learning objectives
- learning campaign components, including content blocks, lessons, activities, assessments, and supporting resources
- evaluation strategies, specifically how you will know the learners have met the learning objectives
- a detailed project implementation plan.

The design phase, at a high level, is the same for any training program. The process outlined here provides the specific requirements for creating a blended learning campaign. Blended learning is more complex than standalone delivery modalities, and there are a lot of considerations when designing a campaign.

Document the Learning Objectives

As you start to design your blended learning campaign, you will constantly revisit your learning objectives, because they will direct almost all your design decisions—from selection of instructional treatments to assessment strategies to selection of instructional technology for authoring content and delivering lessons.

According to Patti Shank, "Well-written learning objectives form the foundation of any learning experience and set the stage for behavior change and improved performance." Even if you are converting existing learning content to a blended format, you need to spend time validating that your learning objectives are on target. They need to align to the business requirements, as well as support what the learners need to know, what they need to be able to do, and how their behaviors need to change because of the blended learning campaign.

RESOURCE

The more precisely learning objectives are written, the easier it is to write focused instruction. Patti Shank's Writing Better Learning Objectives Job Aid will help you write better, more focused learning objectives for your next blended learning program. (You can access it at http://bit.ly/2EMPHJg.)

PRO TIP

Revisiting learning objectives is worth a meeting with your sponsor. Before you spend any time moving forward in the design process, have a discussion with your client to validate the learning objectives, and articulate how each one supports their business requirements.

After you have drafted and validated your learning objectives, it's time to identify what content is needed to support them and in what order that content needs to be delivered. As you move through this design process, remember to consider each learning objective individually. It can help to imagine that each one is a standalone piece of content. If all a learner had to master was the content associated with that objective, what would the design be?

This is, of course, a bit contrived. Some learning objectives don't make sense when delivered as standalone content; however, the thought exercise does allow you to consider the blend through its component parts. At the end of this section, you'll find examples of three learning objectives, and how their design treatment comes together.

Determine the Instructional Strategy

To design content blocks, start by determining what instructional strategy will help learners achieve the desired level of mastery for the learning objective. The strategy provides the framework for how you are going to address the instructional need expressed by the learning objective. The following are common instructional strategies:

- **Task-based learning** is intended to teach about a specific process or procedure that needs to be completed in a specific sequence. There is a measurable outcome, and often only one correct answer. When the goal is to simply teach a task, task-based learning is often used.
- **Game-based learning** is designed as a game that has defined learning outcomes. It is a powerful strategy when you want learners to make choices, but you are not concerned about mistakes, because learners will have the option of doing the right thing after feedback.
- **Social collaborative learning** is a strategy that is dependent on learners interacting with other learners. They combine their knowledge and experiences to increase their mutual mastery of a learning objective.

- **Problem-based learning** allows learners to attain mastery by attempting to solve an open-ended, pre-established problem, either individually or as a group, based on existing experiences, discussions, and reflection. There is usually a correct answer, but the experience of finding ways to solve the problem is more important than getting to the answer.
- **Project-based learning** is like problem-based learning, with the notable difference that a specific deliverable is expected at the end of the instruction.
- **Inquiry-based learning** (or discovery learning) is designed around individuals developing their own questions or problems, researching the answers, and sharing what they've learned.
- **Case-based learning** is a strategy that provides real-life scenarios to illustrate key learning points. The design points back to the scenario throughout the discussion, and relies on the interaction between learners to move forward through the instruction. This type of learning does take a linear path and, through facilitation, arrives at a pre-determined answer.

These strategies don't have to stand alone; they can be combined. For example, if you want to implement a problem-based instructional strategy, you can do that in a social collaborative way. A strategy gives you direction and a framework for designing your instruction.

As you identify the strategy for each learning objective, you'll probably find that many of them will benefit from a similar approach. Identifying the instructional strategy early gives you a starting point for the narrative of your blended learning campaign.

Identify Content Blocks and Curriculum Sequence

After you've identified the most appropriate instructional strategies for your blended learning campaign, it's time to start chunking your content into individual blocks. These are groups of integrated lessons, activities, assessments, and resources that, when combined, support an individual learning objective.

Let's look closer at each type of resource that composes your learning campaign:

- **Lesson:** This term is used when the audience is actively learning something new, and there is an expectation that there will be an assessment to ensure that knowledge has been transferred or skills obtained.
- **Practice Activity:** A practice activity is the opportunity to practice or use content obtained through a lesson. It reinforces the what was learned.

- **Assessment:** An assessment is an evaluation or checkpoint that ensures the learning has been transferred. It can be a traditional multiple-choice test or on-the-job observation. There is some overlap between an activity and an assessment; however, an assessment can be embedded as a moderated activity (group work) or self-directed (a reflection activity).
- **Resource:** A resource reinforces, reminds, or introduces content. It is reusable, and should be designed to be a performance support tool. Resources can be infographics, short videos, podcasts, social collaborative communities, coaching—anything that supports the learning before and after the formal event.

At this point in the design, you should be thinking about the learner experience. Where will learners interact with the content? When will they need it?

Where Will the Learner Be?

You need to consider the authenticity of your training design early in the design process. Chapter 2 introduced the idea that people can learn in four places: in the classroom, at a desk, on a mobile device while on the go, and on the job. To create the most authentic learning environment, you should design the components of your blended learning campaign to be delivered where the learner will be applying what they have learned.

For example, if you are teaching new instructional designers how to write learning objectives, they'll most likely be doing that work at their desk, so the resources that support this learning design should be deployed to a desktop learning environment.

Conversely, if the blended learning campaign is designed to enable experienced salespeople to sell a new product in a face-to-face environment, it's a good bet that they're relying on mobile devices on a regular basis. Therefore, the most authentic place for salespeople to learn is through their mobile device and, perhaps, in a face-to-face classroom to practice in-person sales skills. This experience can be made even more authentic by engaging the sales manager to observe and evaluate the effectiveness of the salesperson in a real work situation.

When Will the Learner Need the Content?

Instructional designers also need to consider *when* the learning will take place. To start, is the experience formal or informal? Formal events are structured, measurable, and scheduled. Informal learning is less structured and happens at the learner's discretion.

Consider whether the learners will need a formal introduction to the skill in a structured environment before attempting it on their own, or if they can learn it while actively doing the work. Following this thought process can help you more easily determine which "when" is most appropriate for your learners. Selecting an authentic learning environment makes this decision easier. If you select this classroom environment, your "when" is formal, as the time spent learning in a classroom is managed and measurable.

In mobile learning environments and desktop computer learning environments, learning can be either formal or informal. Various technologies allow learners to access content on-demand or formally, providing more flexible delivery options. For example, e-learning or video modules accessed on a mobile device can be on-demand, while scheduled virtual class sessions completed on a desktop computer can take place formally.

On-the-job (OTJ) learning usually calls for an informal learning experience. For example, to learn how to create a new PowerPoint template for a deliverable later in the same week, a learner may seek guidance from a colleague, access an online tutorial, or review an online forum. This less formal OTJ training is just in time because it's accessed at the moment of need.

Applying the When and Where

Learner needs drive the where and when of learning, so they must be considered at the same time. You need to determine both before identifying the instructional techniques and learning technologies you'll use.

The core of every learning experience is the individual learner. Delivery mechanisms and trends are not nearly as important as the individuals participating in your programs. Keep your focus on them and use your where and when choices to meet their needs. Doing so will help you meet the goal of the modern classroom: creating authentic, effective, useful learning experiences.

When designing a formal blended learning campaign, you are addressing that first moment of learning need—when learning something new—and giving learners the opportunity to practice new skills, apply new knowledge, and participate in activities and assessments that will measure their mastery of these skills.

In the traditional model of training, where just one delivery mode is used to support an entire curriculum, all new content would be delivered within a finite period—a two-day workshop, a one-hour webinar, or 30-minute e-learning lesson. Because you only had the learners' attention for a preset amount of time, it was critical that you included everything they needed to know in these confined experiences. One of the biggest advantages of designing blended learning campaigns is the flexibility of the delivery model. You can time release the content in a way that allows learners to absorb, reflect, and apply what they've learned before they have to learn something else.

To ensure that the resources you create to support your blended learning campaign continue to be valuable, consider other moments of learning need—specifically, when learners are applying what they've learned and when things go wrong. As you identify resources to use in the formal campaign, contemplate how those same resources can be used to extend the learning. For example, instead of listing the steps for creating a meeting agenda on a presentation slide, create an infographic and use that to teach. This gives the learners a distinct learning asset upon which they can draw when they actually need to create an agenda on the job, which is much more useful than searching for slide 67 of 222 in a presentation deck. And instead of creating a five-minute lecture on how to manage a difficult meeting participant, why not design a short, animated video? They can use it to learn the new content during the formal event, and then refer to it when prepping for their meeting. Providing a tool that will be used over and over will make up for the time it takes to create it.

By anticipating when the learners need a refresher or reminder, and incorporating those needs into your learning design, you will create a rich and valuable learning experience that won't end when the LMS issues a completion certificate.

Identify Instructional Techniques

Before you pick the technologies to deploy each content block, you need to consider what instructional techniques you should use to implement the desired instructional strategy. Instructional techniques are often implemented as activities—they are the "how you get there" part of the puzzle. Many instructional techniques are familiar to both instructional designers and learners, and can be deployed with many different technologies.

The intent and basic design for creating techniques should be similar no matter what the overarching instructional strategy is, or what the instructional technology used. Common techniques include:

- lectures, whether live, recorded, or print on-screen
- brainstorming between learners
- simulations, including role play and immersive learning (augmented and virtual reality)
- gamification, including leader boards and badging
- case studies, including examples that illustrate key points
- moderated discussions, including in-person discussions and moderated discussion boards.

Identify Instructional Technologies

At this point in the design process you'll finally start making decisions about which instructional technologies will support each content block. This may be different from the approach you normally take when designing instruction; instructional technology is often selected prior to any instructional design taking place. For example, this request may seem familiar to you: "We want our eight-hour project management class converted to a half-day virtual classroom session."

When designing blended learning campaigns, it's critical that you go through the process of validating learning objectives, identifying content blocks, and identifying potential instructional strategies and techniques before making your technology selection. If you start with the technology, you limit your options and lose out on all that a blend has to offer.

The instructional technology deploys the content to the learners. You should select a technology for each individual content block that supports the techniques you want to use for that block, as well as the overall instructional strategy. However, you're not selecting a single technology for all content blocks. Instead of discussing different types of software, this book discusses six different categories of instructional technologies:

- **Technologies that support knowledge and content distribution.** These technologies are used to create learning resources such as documents, job aids, presentations, e-learning modules, screencasts, videos, audio recordings, infographics, and course maps.

- **Technologies that support communication and interaction.** These tools are used to reach your learners through email, announcements, and any other outreach broadcast media, along with discussion forums, chat, collaboration, and virtual classroom meeting technologies. Interactions are managed in a structured way, and discussions are often moderated.

- **Technologies that support social interactions, collaboration, and community building.** As you encourage individuals to learn from one another, you will need technologies that are more community oriented. For example, while creating a community of practice or personal learning network is not a project goal or objective, you know that putting one in place will promote knowledge and skill acquisition in your learners' moments of need. These social and community tools and apps can help.

- **Technologies that support assessment and evaluation.** These technologies are used to measure, validate, forecast, and inform, focusing on quantifying or qualifying the impact of learning. They include tools that support tests, surveys, and assignments, and can help inform the effectiveness of your learning solutions and measure the impact learning has on the business.

- **Tools that support immersive learning experiences.** Simulations have been around for a long time, but newer technologies, such as virtual reality and augmented reality, enable these experiences on a much lower budget.

- **Tools that support curation.** Curation technologies are used to explore the web to find resources related to specific topics that you can save, reference, or share through other channels. In any blended learning campaign, a curation strategy can improve the outcomes for your learners.

RESOURCE

The e-book *Sorting Through the Edtech Toolbox*, by InSync Training, explores the six categories of instructional technologies in detail, and provides examples of each. (You'll find it at http://bit.ly/2qpWbdN.)

The Role of Collaboration in Technology Selection

Why do you suppose we bring people together to learn? Is it merely so a facilitator can lecture to a multitude of people simultaneously? Or is it to provide opportunities for deeper learning through collaboration, with two or more people practicing new skills and applying new knowledge?

For me, the purpose of bringing people together to learn goes beyond allowing a facilitator to lecture a multitude of people simultaneously. It is so people can collaborate with the facilitator and one another. True learning rarely happens in a vacuum, and collaboration leads organically to deeper understanding and a richer experience.

For example, a salesperson can read an article about (or listen to a lecture on) how storytelling can help increase sales, and get the gist of the idea being shared. But how much more meaningful would it be for that salesperson to collaborate with others on building a story that inspires sales action, practice delivering that story, receive feedback on that story, and provide feedback to others on their stories?

Collaboration helps learners build mental models through practice and application. Mental models are the scaffolding of our internal learning structure, and help us take what we learn in a classroom and apply it in the real-time world of our work. When selecting the most appropriate instructional technology to support an activity, evaluate if collaboration between learners will add to the experience. If the purpose of the activity is to share knowledge, but not apply that knowledge, collaboration may not be necessary. If, however, collaboration between learners will increase the value of the activity, you should consider tools that are much more interactive.

While this may seem obvious, how often have you attended a virtual classroom session that consisted almost entirely of lecture and slides? If you could have just watched the recording of that virtual classroom session, and received the same value, I would argue that that content should have been delivered in an on-demand format. Why go through the hassle of organizing everyone's calendars so they're in the same place at the same time if they're not interacting and collaborating with one another?

If you think collaboration will add value, you then need to decide what type of collaboration makes the best sense. Here are two types to consider:

- **Concurrent collaboration** allows all learners to interact at once (simultaneously). Sometimes, your learners want as much information as possible in real time. Allowing learners to brainstorm, share, and react spontaneously can add real value to certain instructional strategies, including inquiry-based learning and problem-based learning. If you decide concurrent collaboration is the best approach, consider a real-time technology like the virtual classroom or a video chat. Also, remember that blended learning campaigns can include traditional classroom opportunities, too.

- **Consecutive collaboration** allows learners to interact one at a time (serially). Depending on the topic, it may be better for learners to reflect upon or practice what they've learned before collaborating with their peers. If a more thoughtful approach to collaboration is required, consider technologies like discussion boards or learning communities. The challenge with incorporating consecutive collaboration technologies into a formal blended learning campaign is that they take time to moderate, and it is difficult to force people to participate if they are not accustomed to them.

Communities of Learners and People

Engaged learners in a blended learning campaign can develop more meaningful relationships than those in more traditional programs because they get to know one another over a longer period of time and through a variety of communication methods. They learn to trust one another's curiosity and expertise, and eventually form a community of learners. The more engaging the experience is, the more disappointed they are when the class is over and the community disbands.

Instead of losing this enthusiasm and engagement, extend the learning experience by providing ways for the learners to continue collaborating. Use a community tool to group learners into cohorts where they can continue learning from one another, as well as reach outside those cohorts into a larger community of people who share similar experiences and expertise. These individuals can work together, and become mentors to newer members of the community.

TOOL

Do you know what tools you already have? Use the "Instructional Technology Inventory" at the end of this chapter to document what you have in place. Be sure to share with your colleagues, and keep this list up to date.

Map Your Learning Objectives

Let's put this into practice by looking at learning objectives from the ATD Writing for Instructional Design and Training Certificate (Table 3-1). The audience for this blended learning campaign consists of instructional designers who will perform much of this work at their desk. Therefore, the most authentic place to deliver content is at their desks, supplemented with mobile-ready tools to support them while having conversations with clients.

TOOL

To design your own blended learning campaign, use the "Mapping Learning Objectives to Strategies, Techniques, and Technologies" tool at the end of this chapter.

Table 3-1. Example Learning Objective Mapped to a Blended Program

Objective	How It Maps
Learning Objective	Apply persuasive writing techniques when creating needs assessment reports, and design documents that effectively articulate your training solution.
Instructional Strategy	Learners will individually create the needs assessment reports and design documents (project-based learning).
Lesson Content and Instructional Techniques	New content for learners may include: • What are persuasive writing techniques? • How are they evaluated? Techniques would include a combination of case studies, brainstorming, and lecture.
Activities	Activities that support this objective may include: • Critiquing existing needs assessment reports and design documents • Creating needs assessment reports and design documents that use persuasive writing techniques
Assessments	Assessments that support this objective may include: • Review of learner-created documents by a peer using a rubric • On-the-job discussion with a training client using these documents
Resources	Possible resources that support this objective include: • Templates of needs assessment reports and design documents • A self-evaluation rubric to be used on the job • A three-minute animated video explaining persuasive writing techniques
Instructional Technologies	Potential technologies to deploy resources include: • Documents to create and deploy templates and rubrics • An authoring tool to create video • The virtual classroom to support lecture, case studies, and brainstorming

Manage Instructional Complexity With a Course Map

A blended learning campaign is complex. Occurring over weeks or months, it can include a combination of live and self-directed lessons, activities, and assessments. It's supported by many resources, including job aids, videos, blog posts, and podcasts. To manage the instructional complexity of a blend, you should create a visual course map. Some benefits of creating a course map include:

- **Charting the journey:** Course maps explain the journey for learners, helping them get started, find (and stay focused on) their learning pathway, and determine what it will take to complete the journey.
- **Organizing and visualizing curricula:** Course maps organize and visualize the curricula so that learners and stakeholders can understand the relationships between knowledge and skill activities, sequence of learning, assessments, and learning outcomes.
- **Aiding the instructional design process:** Course maps aid the instructional design process by making it easy to identify gaps or redundancies in the blended learning curriculum, while also helping to align activities to goals and objectives.
- **Providing an overview of transitions:** Course maps provide an excellent overview of transitions through the curriculum from simple to more complex concepts and applications within the blended learning experience.

For the implementation team, creating a course map during the design phase will provide a road map of the program deliverables, and serve as a communication tool when discussing the development and implementation of the blended learning campaign with stakeholders. As the design evolves, the course map should be updated and used as a project management tool. The design of the visual should equalize the value of all the resources and events supporting the blended learning campaign. Live lessons and self-directed lessons should be represented equivalently.

For learners, the course map connects the dots between the content blocks. It serves as an overview of the entire blended learning campaign, a checklist to track lesson completion, and a time management tool. You may even consider making the course map the homepage for the program, linking each resource and lesson listed to the actual resource or lesson online.

The course map is a critical management tool, both for the implementation team and for your learners. It makes a potentially overwhelming experience easy to navigate and less onerous to complete.

TOOL

Reference the "Creating a Course Map" tool at the end of this chapter for guidance on how to create a course map. It also provides a variety of examples.

Plan to Extend the Learning

Most learning occurs outside formal training. But that does not mean you cannot influence your learners. Your challenge is how to stay involved and relevant after the formal blended learning campaign is over, once learners start to learn informally.

PRO TIP

In the article "Finding the Value in Informal Learning," Sarah Danzl (2016) quotes Todd Tauber, vice president of product marketing at the learning platform Degreed, who said: "You can't control what people do, but you can control the environment you provide them. Give learners easy access to the best resources, including other peers." (You can find the article at http://bit.ly/2DE4F3X.)

Make Campaign Resources Useful

When learners attend a traditionally delivered class, they expect to leave with paper—a participant guide and copies of the slides, at the very least. So, what should learners expect from a blended learning campaign?

Instead of providing slides and guides, rely on the tools you want learners to use back on the job. Teach using job aids, checklists, infographics, and videos, and encourage learners to refer to these resources in specific moments of need. A checklist for effective meeting planning is much more useful than a list of bullet points on a slide. So, teach to the checklist (and other resources), and make sure all the resources are always available and up to date.

Embed Resources in the Flow of Work

After creating a toolkit of useful resources and instructing learners how to use them during the formal campaign, it's important to make them accessible when the learners require them. Anticipate when people will need a tool, and embed that tool in the workflow. This makes the formal content reusable as performance support, allowing learners to use it informally.

Propose the Recommended Blended Learning Campaign Design

Because complex blended learning is so new to organizations, it's important to share the design with all your stakeholders.

Create a detailed report that contains the products of the design phase, including:

- finalized learning objectives, illustrating how they support business requirements
- the design of the initial content blocks and supporting instructional strategies, techniques, and technologies
- a detailed course map illustrating the flow of the campaign, its timing, and the supporting resources
- an extended learning plan to illustrate the added value to the business, due to its investment in the development of the recommended resources.

In addition to the design, your proposal should include:

- Technology recommendations for hardware, software, and devices. What do you have? What do you need to buy?
- Content development recommendations. What should you build in-house? What should you outsource, to whom, and why?
- Recommendations for who should be on the development and pilot teams.
- A timeline for development and the pilot.
- A budget for the development and implementation of the design through the pilot stage.

Once finalized, this design plan will serve as the launch pad for the content strategy and rollout. Use it to present the results of your needs assessment and design, as well as your take on the business requirements and results of the organizational readiness analysis.

Remember, your stakeholders and sponsors likely won't have a background in instructional design; rather, they are aligned with the business. To get buy-in on your direction, you need to craft your message in a way that resonates with your stakeholders, who have a very clear vision of what they want the initiative to accomplish. They will look on the initiative as an allocation of resources that could be directed at another project, so you need to prove the program's value.

Your presentation should begin with showing how identified organizational needs will be met by your proposed direction. Use your course map to provide a visual to facilitate the conversation. Also, remember to discuss any ancillary benefits that may result, such as enhanced collaboration between teams or the adoption of new technologies. Include any details about how this design will distinguish itself.

Ask your stakeholders for documented agreement that you are moving in the right direction. If your understanding of the business requirements is not the same as theirs, your blended learning campaign will not be successful.

What's Next?

You've created a design. And you've probably realized that the implementation of this design is more complex than the implementation of a more traditionally delivered program. How do you manage all the moving parts?

To ensure your blended learning program is successful, and continues to be successful over multiple deliveries, you need to create a plan to strategically manage the content so it is always up to date and continues to be useful. You also need to curate new content so that the program and its component parts never feel outdated. Your implementation plan also needs to address the people part of the blend, including the evolving roles of facilitators, producers, and managers. Chapter 4 addresses these critical elements of blended learning implementation.

Questions to Explore

- Do you know how the design of your blended learning program supports critical learning outcomes?
- Did you link business requirements to training needs? How?
- Do you think your organization is ready to implement modern blended learning? Why or why not?
- When converting an existing program to a blended learning campaign, how should the learning objectives change?
- How complex will your blend be? What might keep it from being successful?

Tools for Support

Business Requirements Worksheet

As you explore the need for a specific blended learning campaign, you should document needs specific to your customer. In addition to client-specific needs, be sure to ask how the desired learning solution can meet the business outcome. To help your client prepare, share this worksheet prior to the design kick-off meeting, and provide context for why the information is critical to the project.

1. Goals and Objectives

What are the overall goals and specific objectives of the blended learning initiative?

2. Purpose and Scope

What problems or performance improvements will the blended learning initiative target and serve to solve?

3. Learning Culture

How committed is the organization to supporting and facilitating the design, development, delivery, and management of the blended learning initiative?

4. Stakeholder Input

How engaged or involved are key stakeholders in the design, development, delivery, or management of blended learning?

5. Target Audience

Who are the target learners or groups?

6. Impact and Success

What processes, procedures, or performances will benefit directly from the successful implementation of the blended learning initiative?

7. Team Allocation

Which organizational teams will be involved in the design, development, delivery, and management of the blended learning initiative?

8. Existing Resources

What resources currently exist that can support the design, development, delivery, and management of the blended learning initiative?

9. Scoping Additional Resources

What methods are in place to scope out and acquire additional resources as needed to support the blended learning initiative?

10. Timing and Logistics

Is there a set calendar or project schedule for each phase of the blended learning initiative?

11. Significant Priorities

How will the organization determine resource, budget, calendar, and personnel priorities related to the blended learning initiative?

12. Workflow Approval

What are the process and communication protocols for approval in the design, development, delivery, and management phases of the blended learning initiative?

13. Evident Challenges

What challenges stand out as possible constraints to the success of the blended learning initiative?

Blended Learning Organizational Readiness Assessment

Use this tool to determine how prepared your organization is to implement a blended learning program. Any components that you indicate as "not yet prepared" pose a potential risk, and you should discuss them with your client and with the implementation team. Document your opinions and your discussions, and then find ways to evolve your organization's readiness as part of your process.

Readiness Area: Learning Culture

	Not Yet Prepared	Moderately Prepared	Highly Prepared
Learning is valued, no matter how it is delivered.	The organization is not fully committed to supporting and facilitating learning.	The organization is committed to supporting and facilitating learning through existing delivery channels and approaches.	The organization is committed to supporting and facilitating learning through any delivery channel or approach that promotes information exchange, skill acquisition, and knowledge mastery.
Individuals have protected time to learn.	Individuals are not guided to set aside protected time for learning events and activities.	Individuals are guided to set aside protected time for formal learning events and activities.	Individuals are guided to set aside protected time for formal and informal learning events and activities.
Individuals can learn at their desks without being interrupted.	Individuals are not comfortable learning at their desks.	Individuals can learn at their desks, but would benefit from learning how to avoid distraction and manage interruptions.	Individuals can learn at their desks, and know how to avoid distraction and manage interruptions.
Individual learning paths are defined.	Individual learning paths are not discussed or considered.	Individual learning paths (and preferred modes of delivery and interaction) are defined.	Individual learning paths are defined based on training needs and preferred modes of delivery and interaction.

	Not Yet Prepared	Moderately Prepared	Highly Prepared
Individuals are empowered to manage their own learning.	Individuals do not have support or guidance on the design or implementation of self-directed learning plans.	Individuals have support and guidance on the design and implementation of self-directed learning plans.	Individuals have support and guidance on the design and implementation of self-directed learning plans and personal learning networks.
Community-based knowledge sharing is allowed.	Community-based knowledge sharing is not allowed.	Community-based knowledge sharing is allowed.	Community-based knowledge sharing is considered essential, with easy access to shared knowledge resources and avenues for learner feedback and comments.
Reward systems are in place for learner initiative.	Learners do not receive any incentives for participating in learning initiatives.	Learners receive incentives for participating in formal learning initiatives.	Learners are receive incentives for participating in formal and informal learning initiatives.

Readiness Area: Organizational Support

	Not Yet Prepared	Moderately Prepared	Highly Prepared
The organization is actively engaged in moving through the change curve for blended learning adoption.	The organization is not aware of the change curve for blended learning adoption.	The organization is committed to evaluating where they are on the change curve for blended learning adoption.	The organization is committed to evaluating where they are on the change curve for blended learning adoption, and providing guidance and support for moving individuals and groups toward commitment.
Help desk support is available to assist learners and training team members when they need it.	No help desk support services are available.	Help desk support services are available for learners and training team members (e.g., individual consultations, limited call center hours, and reference materials).	Robust help desk support services are available for learners and training team members (e.g., individual consultations, expanded call center hours, a searchable community knowledge base, and easy to access reference materials).
Managers are engaged in blended learning.	Managers are not engaged or involved in the design, development, or delivery of blended learning.	Managers are partially engaged in the design, development, and delivery of blended learning, providing input as needed.	Managers are fully engaged in the design, development, and delivery of blended learning, driving these processes toward the achievement of organizational goals.
The organization understands, values, and implements content strategy.	Content strategy is not part of the blended learning design process.	Content strategy is part of the blended learning design process. Resources are provided to support the implementation.	Content strategy is an integral part of the blended learning design process. Resources are provided to support the implementation, and it is integrated into the blended learning design.

	Not Yet Prepared	Moderately Prepared	Highly Prepared
The budgeting process for learning projects is easy to understand and implement.	The budgeting process has not been detailed.	The budgeting process has been detailed for each project phase.	There is a detailed budgeting process that includes examples and accompanying guidelines for each project phase.
There are dedicated resources supporting blended learning administration.	The administration of blended learning is not an important function of the organization.	The administration of blended learning is an important function of the organization, but additional support is necessary to staff and finance.	The administration of blended learning is an essential function of the organization, and it is supported by financial and human resources.
There is a plan to make sure learning is applied on the job.	There is no plan in place to follow through with participants to see whether learning is applied on the job.	There is a plan to follow through with participants to see whether learning is applied on the job.	The organization regularly follows through with participants to see whether learning is applied on the job.

Readiness Area: Technology Tools and Infrastructure

	Not Yet Prepared	Moderately Prepared	Highly Prepared
The LMS is set up to support blended learning.	The LMS does not support every delivery method and approach in the blended learning program.	The LMS supports every delivery method and approach in the blended learning program.	The LMS supports every delivery method and approach in the blended learning program. Learners have easy access to all blended learning components, including single sign-on access.
Authoring tools and associated licenses have been procured.	A limited selection authoring tools needed to design, develop, and deliver blended learning materials are available and licensed for use.	All authoring tools needed to design, develop, and deliver blended learning materials are available and licensed for individual use.	All authoring tools needed to design, develop, and deliver blended learning materials are available and licensed for teams to use. A reporting mechanism keeps track of tools, costs, and license expiration dates.
Robust virtual classroom tools are available for use within blended learning programs.	No virtual classroom tool is available, or it's available in a very limited application that does not fully support engagement in the virtual classroom.	Virtual classroom tools are available, including whiteboard, chat, video, screen sharing, application sharing, polls, and breakout session capabilities.	A stable, supported set of virtual classroom tools are available, including whiteboard, chat, video, screen sharing, application sharing, polls, and breakout session capabilities.
There is a methodology in place for piloting new instructional technologies.	There is no process or methodology in place for piloting new instructional technologies	There is a flexible process in place for piloting new technologies by teams involved in the design, development, and delivery of blended learning. Guidance is available to work through the process.	An established protocol exists for piloting new and emerging technologies. Pilot success criteria are established and communicated, scope and duration are well defined, and administrative infrastructure is in place to guide the initiative and minimize associated risks.

Readiness Area: Training Team Readiness

	Not Yet Prepared	Moderately Prepared	Highly Prepared
The training team has the skills they need to be successful.	Individuals involved in the design, development, delivery, and management of blended learning do not have the skills needed to be productive and successful.	Individuals involved in the design, development, delivery, and management of blended learning have the skills needed to be productive.	Individuals involved in the design, development, delivery, and management of blended learning have the skills needed to be productive and successful.
The organization is willing to invest in continuing education for the training team.	The organization has no plans for evaluating or supporting the training team's continuing education needs.	The organization evaluates continuing education needs on an annual basis, and invests in upskilling training for team members when requested.	The organization is committed to continuously evaluating and upskilling training for team members, and communicating the value of how individual skills fit into the overall picture.
The training team has established communication channels and protocols.	There are no internal or external communication channels or protocols in place for training team members.	Internal and external communication channels and protocols are in place and usually followed.	Internal and external communication channels and protocols are in place and consistently followed, including reporting channels for key stakeholders.
There are enough redundancies in place if a resource is not available.	No training team member resource redundancies are in place.	A coverage plan is in place for training team member resource outages or vacancies.	Training team members have been cross-trained, adding functional redundancy to the team. There is a detailed coverage plan for resource unavailability or vacancies, including funding for outsourcing.

Readiness Area: Learner Readiness

	Not Yet Prepared	Moderately Prepared	Highly Prepared
Learners have access to the appropriate devices and equipment to fully participate.	Learners do not have access to devices that support modes of delivery and participation within blended learning programs.	Learners have access to devices that support some modes of delivery and participation within blended learning programs.	Learners have access to devices that support all modes of delivery and participation within blended learning programs. Any necessary operating system versions or application updates are addressed in advance.
Training is available for learners new to the blended learning environment.	No introductory training is in place to support learners new to the blended learning environment.	Learners who are new to blended learning have access to introductory training.	Learners who are new to blended learning have access to introductory training that models the blended learning experience, offering formal, informal, and social learning elements to support the transition.
Learners know what and why they need to learn.	The organization doesn't communicate information about what learners will be learning, or why they are being asked to participate in the blended learning program.	Learners receive clear and timely information related to what they will be learning, and why they are being asked to participate in the blended learning program.	Learners receive clear and timely information related to what they will be learning, and why they are being asked to participate in the blended learning program. This communication demonstrates the alignment of specific blended learning components with set learning goals and objectives.

	Not Yet Prepared	Moderately Prepared	Highly Prepared
Communication channels and protocols are in place to prepare and engage learners.	No communication channels or protocols are established to prepare learners for blended learning programs.	Communication channels and protocols are established to prepare learners for blended learning programs (e.g., scheduled events, activities, interactions, and content release cycles).	Communication channels and protocols are established and implemented to prepare learners for blended learning programs (e.g., scheduled events, activities, interactions, and content release cycles). Reminders and new content alerts are sent on a regular basis to engage learners and connect them with instructors, peers, mentors, and key influencers.

Adapted with permission from InSync Training

Instructional Technology Inventory

Do you know what tools you already have ready to use? Use this worksheet to document what you have in place. Be sure to share with your colleagues, and keep this list up to date.

Knowledge and Content

These are the materials that you create, curate, and deliver for your learners to access fall into the category of knowledge and content. Use these tools to create learning assets such as job aids, presentations, e-learning modules, screencasts, videos, audio recordings, infographics, course maps, and the like.

Creating Documents	Creating Presentations	Creating Graphics
• Microsoft Office Suite • Google Docs • Open Office • Adobe Acrobat • Adobe InDesign • Framemaker • CloudOn • iWork	• PowerPoint • Keynote • Prezi • Google Slides • Clear Slide • Slide Bean • slides.com • Haiku Dec • DeskSet • Swipe	• Adobe Photoshop • Fireworks • Canva • Piktochart • Tableau • www.istockphoto.com • www.123rf.com • www.depositphotos.com • Noun Project • UnSplash
Creating E-Learning	**Creating Audio**	**Creating Video**
• Captivate • Lectora • Camtasia • Articulate • Adobe Presenter • Office Mix • PlayPosit	• Zencastr • Audacity • Adobe Audition • Just Press Record • Google Voice to Text	• PowToon • Office Mix • Camtasia • VideoScribe • Adobe Spark • VeeScope
Creating Screencasting		
• Captivate • Camtasia • Office Mix • Jing • Vittle		

Notes:

Communication and Interaction

You can use these tools and apps to reach your learners through email, announcements, or any other outreach broadcast media, along with discussion forums, chat, collaboration, and virtual classroom meeting tools and apps.

Communication	Broadcasting	Interaction
• Email • Phone • Text • WhatsApp • Google Hangouts • mail.com	• Moodle • Totara • Slack • LinkedIn • Yammer	• Skype • Phone • Slack • LMS discussion forums • Chat feature within live sessions • Zoom meeting

Notes:

Social and Community

Some of the tools and apps here stretch across categories. You use social media to share content, communicate, interact, and collaborate. Sometimes creating a community of practice or personal learning network is not a project goal or objective, but you know that putting one in place will certainly promote knowledge and skill acquisition in our learners' moments of need. These social and community tools and apps can help us do just that.

Features to Look for:
• Profiles • Connections • Groups • Messages • Sharing • Updates • Search

Notes:

Assessment and Evaluation

These tools focus on quantifying or qualifying the impact of learning. You can use this array of tech tools and apps for tests, surveys, and assignments, as well as for determining the value of your learning initiatives. For some, these tools inform the effectiveness of your learning solutions, for others these tools indicate your business impact. Simply put, you can use them to measure, validate, forecast, and inform.

Surveys	Tests and Quizzes	Assignments
• Zoho • Survey Monkey	• Moodle • Totara • Blackboard • Bridge • WP Quiz • Quiz and Survey Master	• What's built into the LMS

Notes:

Virtual and Augmented Reality

These tools and apps enable you to create immersive learning experiences for your learners. Simulations have been around for a long time, but newer tools and apps enable you to engage your learners in immersive experiences on a much lower budget. What was once a highly segmented toolset is now available for you to explore and integrate into your own practices.

Virtual Reality	Augmented Reality
• Google Cardboard • InMind VR • Within VR • Insta360 Camera	• Google Cardboard • Star Walk • Hidden Sky • Pokemon GO • Insta360 Camera

Notes:

Curation

You can use these tools and apps to explore the web to find resources related to specific topics that you can save, reference, or share through other channels. In any modern blended learning program, a curation strategy can improve the outcomes for your learners.

RSS Feed Readers	Content Aggregators
• Feedly • Feeder	• Flipboard • Storify
Curation List Tools	**Full Curation Engine**
• eLink • list.ly	• Curata • Anders Pink

Notes:

Adapted with permission from InSync Training.

Mapping Learning Objectives to Strategies, Techniques, and Technologies

To help in the design of your own blended learning campaign, use this tool to map your learning objectives to strategies, techniques, and technologies.

Learning Objective	
Instructional Strategy	
Lesson Content and Instructional Techniques	
Activities	
Assessments	
Resources	
Instructional Technologies	

Creating a Course Map

A course map is a visual representation of the courses or learning activities specific to an entire blended learning experience. The course map provides an overview of the entire blended curriculum by explaining the sequence of events, the types of learning activities, the anticipated length for each activity, and an indication of when the activity will take place. Just as you would rely on a map to guide your way to a specific destination, the course map can be designed to guide learners on the pathway of their learning journeys.

What Are the Elements of a Course Map?

There are no hard and fast rules in developing a course map. Course maps can be static or interactive. A static version can be printed or used in a slide, and an interactive version can be created for a course website to aid in curriculum navigation by participants. Other areas and details can be added depending on the type of blended learning you are creating and the level of complexity within your curriculum.

Every course map will be different, as there are different elements within the design of any blended learning experience. As you build your course map, consider focusing on the areas in the following table.

Element	Description
Topics	These are the areas of focus within the learning journey.
Time	This is the time expected to complete each topic (usually expressed in minutes).
Objectives	These are the learning or performance objective(s) being addressed
Elements	This is the content or teaching points aligned to the objectives.
Methods	These are the approaches and activities approaches used to instruct the topic.
Resources	This encompasses all resources available to support the topic or course.

What Tools Can I Use to Create a Course Map?

Creating a course map is a simple process, and you can create a template without having detailed content for the focus areas you choose to include. You can use a word processing or spreadsheet application for a table format, a mind-mapping application for a flowing format, or a drawing application for a more complex visual representation.

Try starting with a simple sketch on paper to guide your process. As you do this, keep in mind that you will want to explore ways to differentiate the types of learning events that will be taking place. After you sketch things out, translate the diagram into a format that is easy to understand—a format that makes it easy for you to paint a picture or tell a story about the pathways you want your learners to follow.

Remember, the goal is to design a visual representation of the blended learning journey that will inform learners on what to expect before, during, and after the learning experience.

Design Tips

Keep the following tips in mind when creating your course map:

- **Keep it simple:** Make it clear, concise, and visually easy to read and understand.
- **It's in the details:** Provide enough detail to allow trainers, learners, and other stakeholders to quickly grasp the requirements and learning outcomes.
- **Tell a story:** If the sequence of the curriculum alone does not paint a full enough picture, include a narrative to entice and guide learners on their journey. Make sure you highlight the resources that learners will need to complete the blended learning experience.
- **The fine print:** Be sure to visually differentiate materials that will be self-paced and those scheduled at a specific time. If there are elective elements included, be sure that learners know what is required, and what is optional. If you need to provide further context, consider using footnotes to identify conditional requirements for the curriculum.
- **Check, please:** Create a checklist to go along with the course map to help guide participants on their learning journey.
- **What time is it?** Include time management tips and tools (or link to them) within the course map.

Conclusion

Creating a course map is part of the instructional design process. Seeing the curriculum mapped out enables you to better balance the blend, create a learning journey in alignment with stated objectives, and guide the learners on their pathways to success.

Remember to integrate the course map into every learning event within the blended learning solution to be sure that learners know where they are, where they are going, and how they are progressing within their learning journey.

The example below details the four-week curriculums, the content pieces needed for each step, and the milestones along the way.

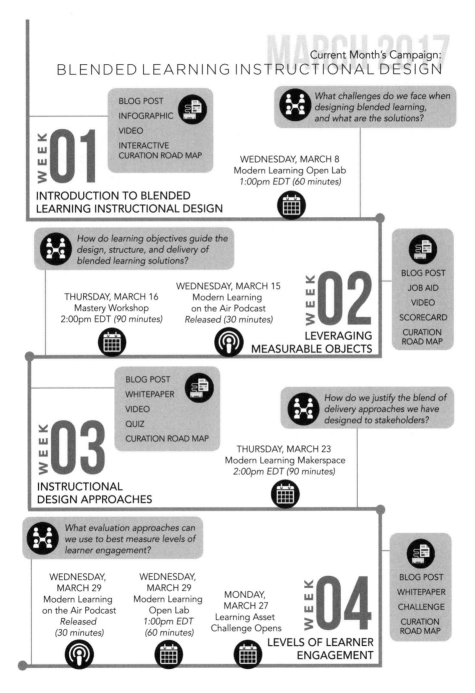

Adapted with permission from InSync Training

Additional Resources

Bersin, J. 2017. "The Disruption of Digital Learning: Ten Things We Have Learned." Josh Bersin blog, March 27. http://joshbersin.com/2017/03/the-disruption-of-digital-learning-ten-things-we-have-learned.

Brandon Hall Group. 2016. *State of Learning and Development 2016: Ready to Evolve.* Delray Beach, FL: Brandon Hall Group. https://trainingmag.com/state-learning-and-development-2016-ready-evolve.

Danzl, S. 2016. "Finding the Value in Informal Learning." ATD Career Development Blog, October 19. www.td.org/insights/finding-the-value-in-informal-learning.

Shank, P. n.d. "Writing Better Learning Objectives Job Aid." Digital Resource. www.td.org/job-aid-tools/writing-better-learning-objectives-job-aid.

4

Implementing the Plan: How Do You Execute an Effective Blended Learning Program?

In This Chapter

- The impact of the content strategy plan
- The roles of the facilitator and producer
- How to curate content for the blend
- Why you need to engage managers

Y ou can design your blended learning campaign in infinite ways as long as you've synced your instructional strategies, techniques, and technologies. However, as chapter 3 showed, a strong focus on business requirements and organizational readiness encourages the adoption of a modern workplace learning mindset and strengthens the partnership between the talent development function and the business. And yet, even if you design the perfect blend, your campaign can still come crashing down if you haven't been deliberate in how you implement your blend. This chapter sets out to show how you can be successful.

Create the Content Strategy Plan

It's time to create the content. Chances are, different people on your team will be responsible for authoring different resources, depending on their expertise and training. Your role as the learning experience architect is to manage the content strategy plan.

The content strategy process can inform and guide the instructional design process, according to learning experience designer Phylise Banner (2017): "When we design blended learning, we need to take the same who, what, where, when, and why into consideration (in alignment with objectives) before we start creating content, or using what we already have. Then we need to inventory what we have, audit (assess the value of) what we find, and then build what we don't yet have."

Content strategy throws its arms around every associated piece that you need to implement an instructional strategy. It's about putting the pieces together, keeping them together, and knowing when to let things go and when to add new content.

Components of the Content Strategy Plan

A lot of careful thinking and planning goes into creating a balanced blend—you're combining different content types at different times to meet different objectives for different people. The instructional design sets the stage for the content strategy, but the strategy is the true blueprint for your campaign. This comes in handy when you're developing, delivering, producing, facilitating, managing, and assessing modern blended learning. The content strategy plan should address content substance, structure, workflow, and governance.

Content Substance

As you begin to develop a training initiative, you need to identify what content already exists, and from what sources you will get or create new content. When considering content substance, always document:

- What content do you have?
- What purpose is it serving?

Content Structure

When you organized your learning objectives into content blocks and identified the resources you would use to support those blocks, you started to create the content structure. When you sequenced the resources into a course map, you continued that process. When considering content structure, always document:

- How will you organize the content?
- What content takes priority? (Is any piece more important than other content?)
- How will you deliver the content?
- How will individual content resources fit into the overall picture?

Content Workflow

It's probably obvious that we need to create the content for now, but who keeps track of changes six months from now? This is especially important for a modern blended learning campaign because it is meant to support learners well after the formal learning is over. Learners need to trust that content is always up to date.

When considering content workflow, always document:

- What do you need to support the content's design, development, delivery, and so on?
- What do you need to maintain and update the content?
- Which processes or people do you need to put into place to assure delivery and ongoing support?
- What is the content life cycle? How often does each resource need to be reviewed and updated?

Content Governance

Content governance answers the question, "Who owns the content?" This is critical in a blend with so many moving parts and so many people involved in development. The most frustrating, and perhaps the most damaging, part of the development process is review by committee. For example, five different people provide five different opinions, and no one is willing to take ownership. Who is correct? That needs to be determined up front, and everyone needs to agree. Authored e-learning content and pre-scripted videos can be very expensive to change after the fact.

This is also the step most likely to slow down the process. Getting input from too many people often results in missed deadlines and can have a critical impact on the timeline.

When considering content governance, always document:

- Who makes decisions about content?
- Who has authority to make changes?
- Who has final say?
- Who manages the communication flow?

TOOL

The "Content Strategy Planning" tool at the end of this chapter will help you manage content substance, structure, workflow, and governance.

The Impact of the Content Strategy Plan

An effective content strategy is one that is invisible and integrated. Does anyone look at a building's blueprints? No, they simply experience the building. When content strategy is done well, no one knows that it's there—or if they do, they're too busy enjoying the experience to think about it. When you don't have content strategy, things can fall through the cracks, you can miss pieces, and the learner experience is negatively affected. A content strategy mindset is replicable and recorded. It champions accountability.

Managing the Facilitation Plan

A strategic facilitation plan is just as critical to implementing a blended learning campaign as the instructional design and the content strategy. That's because facilitating a blended experience is not just about delivering content; it is also about managing the experience. The concept of facilitating a blend is quite different because the facilitator is responsible for:

PRO TIP

You know the content strategy is working if the design implementation works.

- managing live virtual classroom lessons
- moderating social experiences

- supporting self-directed lessons
- curating content
- providing virtual coaching and mentoring.

Facilitators don't just need expertise regarding the content; they need to be experts at integrating technology, content, and support.

The Role of the Facilitator

The facilitator plays a vital role in ensuring that learners are successful. Learners want to develop a personal rapport with the facilitator, and this is especially true in a blended learning campaign because the facilitator acts as an anchor, reassuring learners that support, reinforcement, and assessment are readily available.

However, being an effective facilitator doesn't mean excessively communicating with email messages and lectures. Instead, they must create a learner-centered environment that moves the focus away from themselves and the technology and toward the content and the learners. Effective facilitators also motivate learners, create opportunities for learners to collaborate, blend the experience and technology, and ensure the technology is usable.

Motivate Learners

Virtual classroom components provide a flexible alternative to in-person learning sessions. However, it's important to remember that including live online events in blended learning campaigns creates a markedly different experience for learners. While they still join their peers to learn from an expert facilitator, the virtual environment can leave learners feeling isolated because they aren't coming together in a single room with a facilitator at the front of the class. This isolation can be compounded when learners don't know to whom or how to reach out when they have a question about content, a session, or required coursework.

One way to combat this is by positioning the facilitator at a central contact point, which can help to humanize the digital learning experience. There are many was virtual facilitators can make themselves virtually visible. My best practices include conducting skill and knowledge assessments, offering recognition of learner work and progress, and encouraging collaboration and ongoing relationships within the program.

With the right skills, virtual classroom facilitators can motivate learners to not only engage in the virtual classroom elements, but to succeed throughout the blend.

Create Opportunities for Learners to Collaborate

Even when you intentionally include collaboration opportunities in a program, facilitators can further encourage social learning. Prompting learners to participate in virtual sessions as frequently as possible creates active, engaging events. It's of paramount importance that facilitators minimize lecture time because commenting, elaborating, and drawing on learner contributions helps dial up learner engagement.

Limiting virtual classroom tech jargon also lowers learner isolation. When facilitators make a point to focus on the technology, learners can disengage. Instead, make sure virtual facilitators are using learners' names, commenting on the ideas they share in chat, and giving learners activities to work on while they're launching virtual classroom technology elements.

Blend the Experience, Not Just the Technology

Blended learning facilitators have to manage the content and technology to create a cohesive program. This responsibility includes highlighting key connections between self-directed exercises and live learning events, both of which are required for success in blended learning curricula. It is important that facilitators purposefully incorporate self-directed learning into live events, and keep the lines of communication open before, during, and after sessions to encourage continuing learning connections.

Even technologically savvy learners can get overwhelmed by the technology required for live and self-directed work. So facilitators must create an environment where mastering the technology doesn't interfere with learning key content, and learners can be confident that they can use the platforms and features effectively.

Communicating with learners about the technology and program expectations before the blended learning program begins is an important first step. Mitigating concerns, answering questions, and providing guidance ahead of time minimizes the likelihood that tech issues will take precedence over the skills and knowledge they should be learning.

I advocate for creating a communication plan that not only outlines key program communications, but also includes the timing of each message. I encourage my facilitators to provide detailed set-up instructions for the blended learning technology elements, help desk contact information, and a program orientation. Preemptively answering questions and providing direction develops a level of comfort and confidence that encourages learner success.

Common blended learning challenges arise not from the content, but rather the facilitators lacking mastery of the selected technology. Ask yourself, "Can my facilitators provide learner support and technical assistance clearly and with enough detail that learners can easily follow along?" If you answer "yes," your facilitators are adequately prepared to lead the program. If you answer "no," provide skill-building opportunities for your facilitators to ensure that they feel confident in the virtual working environment.

Facilitator and Producer Teams Ensure Success

In a blend, a facilitator's responsibilities grow exponentially. Is it even possible for one person to successfully manage it all? Often, they can't. Blended programs often benefit from a team teaching approach.

Powerful instructional teams—a facilitator and a producer—maximize program success. Pairing your facilitator with a producer accomplishes two mission-essential goals. It frees the facilitator to focus on teaching the content during live sessions, while the producer deals with the technology. The producer also addresses any technical issues and supports the minutiae of instruction, like communicating deadlines and distributing materials, allowing learners to feel wholly supported. Just remember, communication is key. Learners must know who to turn to when they have a technology issue or need to ask a question about the content.

Many organizations resist team teaching, because it appears more expensive at the outset. Gain buy-in by clearly sharing the benefits of this approach, and providing cost-effective ways of introducing it to your blend. For example, administrative assistants and training coordinators can fill the role of producer. It's also possible to outsource this role to professional resources, which can defray the in-house cost of organizing and managing sessions.

It's a big responsibility, and the facilitator is the face of the entire campaign. Adoption of blended learning isn't just new to your learner audience, it is often a new experience for the people facilitating the process. Ensuring that facilitators are ready to support the process will go a long way toward maximizing the return on investment of time and budget.

Additional Implementation Considerations

When implementing blended learning, there are some other items to consider that will make your campaign even more successful. They include incorporating a content curation strategy and engaging managers in blended learning.

PRO TIP

According to Stephen Walsh (2017) of Anders Pink, curation for learning means:
- finding the best content from multiple sources, usually external content
- filtering it so only the most relevant content makes it through
- sharing it with the right internal audiences, at the right time, in the right places
- adding value to that content with commentary, context, or organization.

Content Curation

With blended learning, we have the latitude to select the content that most effectively and accurately imparts knowledge and builds skills. Content isn't confined to what our instructional designers create on their own. Rather, we can leverage resources from experts in each subject. Content curation involves compiling resources from various sources, and adding commentary and insights to create a learning repository.

One of my favorite analogies for modern learning curation comes from my colleague Phylise Banner. In her blog post "Exploring a Content Curation Practice for Modern Learning," she likens the act of curating resources to creating an art gallery. Mood, context, purpose, and preservation all affect curated learning, just like in a museum environment. From Phylise, I gained the perspective that:

- **Curation begins with defining learning objectives.** For learners to understand the validity and relevance of curated content, it should support and clearly connect to defined learning objectives.

- **Content must have context.** It's not enough to pull resources off the Internet. Curators need to have expert opinions and perspective so they can include commentary that adds weight and clarification to the information. Why does the resource matter? How will it help learners on their learning pathways? How does it support the learning goals? Where can learners find more related information? Learners benefit from the answers to those questions.

- **Make curated resources accessible.** If learners don't know the content is available, it loses its power. Once again, communication takes center stage. Regularly tell learners when and where they can access new curated content, and review it to ensure that the information is still timely and relevant.

- **Take care to preserve the information.** Storing, archiving, and preserving past curated content has merit. Taking the time to review which resources helped learners, which they responded to, and which didn't achieve their goals will help improve the curation process moving forward.

TOOL

Effective curation doesn't just happen. Make the process easier by implementing a content curation plan. Use the "Content Curation Planning Worksheet" tool at the end of this chapter to help you perfect your curation technique.

Manager Engagement

As with any major change management initiative, gaining stakeholder buy-in poses an essential step in the process of implementing a blended learning solution. Without support from managers and stakeholders, it'll be difficult to create momentum around the program and support for the learners.

Managers and co-workers recognize the importance of dedicated classroom training time, but rarely respect other learning moments, such as informal learning, self-guided activities, or even nontraditional formal sessions. This makes it hard for learners to spend time learning at their desks or participating in on-the-job blended learning activities. This culture can prove detrimental to program success. Learners can't succeed if managers don't recognize that learning can take place on the job, at an employee's desk, or even on their mobile device.

While engaging managers in the process is key, instructional designers have to earn managerial support. We can't expect them to buy in to an approach they don't understand. Remember, many employees have never learned in a truly blended model before. It's understandable that they believe the most valuable type of training takes place in a classroom—that's what they're familiar with.

I recommend creating a short, introductory virtual lesson to introduce managers to blended learning. It could include answers to common questions, like:

- Why try blended learning?
- What is a blended learning campaign?

- How can I support my employees participating in a blended program?
- How do I know learning is happening?

Design the lesson so it clearly demonstrates the impact of a well-designed blended learning program. Incorporate informal learning moments, model the communication style you'll use, build in collaboration and opportunities for Q&A, and define learner expectations and program time commitments. In short, share your plans with managers, show them the potential, and include them in the process.

It's also important that you don't stop engaging managers after you've gained initial support. Continue to leverage their expertise by including them in the evaluation element of your program. Since measurable performance improvement won't happen at the end of the program, managers can help you evaluate success. Give them a checklist to observe each learner's on-the-job performance and review ongoing progress and skill building.

PRO TIP

Pollock and Jefferson suggest that managers ask, "What was the most valuable thing you learned?" and "What help do you need to implement what you learned?" immediately after the training. Then several weeks later, managers can ask whether the training has been applied and if it has helped. These simple conversations will demonstrate to the learner that the training was important, and helps validate the manager's investment in the program (Pollock and Jefferson 2012).

TOOL

There is a lot to keep track of. Use the "Blended Learning Implementation Plan Worksheet" tool at the end of this chapter to manage the process.

What's Next

Where do you start when it comes to evaluating a blended learning campaign? The content strategy? The design? The facilitation team? The technology usability and integration? The learner? It's tempting to measure everything and everyone. But, what data are useful?

Chapter 5 looks at the details of the evaluation process, and provides tools to help you collect the data you need in an organized way.

Questions to Explore

- What is your current process for content life cycle maintenance? Will it transfer to blended learning design?
- Is there a role in your organization responsible for content management?
- What does your organization do now to engage managers in learning?

Tools for Support

Content Strategy Planning Tool

As Kristina Halvorson and Melissa Rach (2012) write in *Content Strategy for the Web*, 2nd edition, "Your content strategy defines how an organization (or project) will use content to achieve its objectives and meet its users' needs." To meet your learners' needs, use this job aid to begin your blended learning content strategy by answering these questions:

Mission

- Who are you as an organization or function?
- Who are your learners?
- What do you ultimately want your learners to accomplish?

Content

- What learning content do you already have?
- What is the relative value or appropriateness of existing learning content?
- What gaps exist, and what learning content do you need to develop?
- What tools do you have to support the development of new content?

Substance

- How will learning materials be organized (themes, campaigns, topics, months)?
- How will the design or hierarchy of learning content be determined?
- What system will be used to tag or reference learning content?
- What forms of delivery would be most effective for your organization and learners?
- What tools do you have to support that delivery?

Workflow

- Who is responsible for producing and maintaining existing content?
- What processes need to be in place to move content from development to delivery?

- Who can detail out each of these processes?
- What tools can be used to manage the project workflow?
- What quality assurance and editorial reviews need to be in place?

Governance

- Who are the key decision makers regarding content development and delivery?
- Who determines the learning project priorities?
- What guidelines are in place to handle issues that may arise?
- Who is in charge of the content life cycle and schedule?
- Who is responsible for communicating about changes or results?

Content Curation Planning Worksheet

Curating learning content happens naturally. You find something interesting, and you share it with someone else, along with why you like it, where you found it, what you learned, and why you think that person might find it interesting or useful.

When you curate content for your learners, you can model the process that museum curators follow when developing a gallery show. You can learn from and translate the museum curation process into a content curation process for modern learning by implementing these phases:

- defining purpose, theme and community
- exploring channels and selecting content
- providing a framework of context and annotation
- exhibiting and sharing with the community
- storing, preserving, and archiving.

Use this checklist as a guide for your blended learning content curation process.

Defining Purpose, Theme, and Community

As with every learning experience, you need to begin by defining your objectives; in this case that would be defining the purpose of curating content. Community is a natural consideration when defining the purpose of your curation efforts, and the purpose itself will drive the theme.

☐ The organization is willing to support a structured approach to content curation.

☐ Goals and objectives can be realized through the curation and integration of learning resources.

☐ The community will benefit from up-to-date learning content and resources.

☐ The culture of learning supports sharing links to external resources through a learning management system, social networks, chat, or email.

☐ Content sources that learners currently use to access new information are easily identifiable.

☐ Curation themes or channels can be easily defined around existing target learning content subject areas.

Exploring Channels and Selecting Content

In both the museum world and modern learning landscape, the exploration and content selection process requires an expert eye. Be sure that you understand the topics you intend to curate before you begin the curation process, and always keep the learners and purpose in mind while sifting and selecting the works you intend to share.

- ☐ Learners have the opportunity to share their preferred content channels, sites, and sources.
- ☐ Industry experts and key influencers to follow have been identified.
- ☐ Keywords and phrases have been identified by the learning community, and organized according related themes or learning objectives.
- ☐ A process is in place to identify and filter out unrelated or inappropriate resources.
- ☐ A review schedule is set to revise existing channels and sources, including time to solicit and include input from the community of learners.

Providing a Framework of Context and Annotation

The greatest value of curated content comes through annotation and context. This is where you can add your expertise to the showcase of selected works. In a modern learning scenario, annotation is more than letting learners know where and when content was published; it is wrapping knowledge around the selected content and contextualizing it within the learning framework.

- ☐ Curated content is presented in an easy-to-access format, with a clear title, short overview, and direct link to the associated resource.
- ☐ Learners are made aware of how curated materials relate to specific learning goals and objectives.
- ☐ Contextualization and explanations provide guidance on how curated content is relevant to the learning community.
- ☐ Learners are prompted to follow up on questions or controversies raised in curation annotations.
- ☐ Opportunities are available for learners to further annotate curated resources.

Sharing With the Community

Sharing curated content within learning communities depends on the delivery mechanisms in place. Content can be shared through company blog posts, learning community sites, workplace groups, social media sites, and so on. Be sure to stay consistent with the way curated content is contextualized.

☐ Multiple channels and delivery mechanisms are available for delivering curated resources.

☐ Curated content is easily accessible at any time and from any device.

☐ Learners are aware of any regularly scheduled release or curation update.

☐ Communication methods are established to broadcast or alert learners to new curated content.

☐ When appropriate, specific learner groups are highlighted when they will benefit from targeted curated resources.

☐ Mechanisms are in place to solicit input from learners, including options to "like," "favorite," or rank curated resources.

☐ A review process is in place to remove outdated curated resources.

Storing, Preserving, and Archiving

Curation, in the true sense of the word, is not just about selecting and displaying information, it is about preserving and caring for the information that you share. Preservation and care within the modern learning landscape comes about through thoughtful storage, archiving, and cataloging of curated content.

☐ Records are kept on resources that have been displayed, including when, where, and how they were shared with learners.

☐ A system is in place to tag or catalog curated resources so as to be easily findable.

☐ Data and reports related to curated content are available and easily accessible.

☐ A process is in place to review the quantity and frequency of curated resources accessed, read, shared, or voted on by learners, to inform further curation efforts.

Blended Learning Implementation Plan Worksheet

Blended learning means there is a lot to keep track of. Use this job aid to help manage the process.

Conduct the Needs Analysis

- Complete a needs assessment.
- Document business requirements.
  - » Use the "Business Requirements Worksheet" (chapter 3).
- Create a learning persona to support an audience analysis.
  - » Use the "Creating a Learning Persona" tool (chapter 1).
- Conduct an organizational readiness analysis, including a review of the learning culture, existing organizational support, technology tools and infrastructure, training team readiness, and learner readiness.
  - » Use the "Blended Learning Organizational Readiness Assessment" (chapter 3).
- Document your findings, present to stakeholders, and get official buy-in or approval before moving to the design phase of implementation.

Design the Blended Learning Campaign

- Document learning objectives and get approval before moving to the next step.
- Design the content blocks, including instructional strategy, lessons, activities, and supporting resources.
  - » Use the "Mapping Learning Objectives to Strategies, Techniques, and Technologies" tool in chapter 3.
- Identify what instructional techniques will support each content block.
- Identify what instructional technologies will support each content block.
  - » Use the "Instructional Technology Inventory" tool (chapter 3).
- Create the first version of your course map.
- Document how resources created in the campaign will be useful after the formal learning is complete.

Propose the Recommended Blended Learning Campaign Design

- Document technology recommendations for hardware, software, and devices. What do you have? What do you need to buy?

- Document content development recommendations. What should you build in-house? What should you outsource, to whom, and why?
- Document recommendations for development and pilot team, including administration.
- Document development and pilot timeline.
- Document risks.
- Create a budget.
- Assemble the design and recommendations into a proposal for stakeholders.
- Create and deliver a short presentation that supports your plan.
- Get approval on all aspects of your proposal before moving forward.

Design and Implement the Content Strategy
- Manage content substance, structure, workflow, and governance of your campaign.
  - » Use the "Content Strategy Planning" tool (chapter 4).

Design and Implement the Facilitation Plan
- Identify the facilitation team.
- Prepare the team for the blend.

Create an Evaluation Plan
- Determine what data to collect and who to measure.
- Evaluate your blended learning design.
  - » Use the "Blended Learning Instructional Design Effective Practice Scorecard" tool (chapter 5).
- Measure learner engagement.

Additional Considerations
- Curate your content.
  - » Use the "Content Curation Planning Worksheet" (chapter 4).
- Engage managers.
- Create personalized learning pathways.
  - » Use the "Learning Pathway Planning Worksheet" (chapter 6).

Additional Resources

Banner, P. 2017. "Bringing Content Strategy Into the Blend." *TD*, August. www.td.org /magazines/td-magazine/bringing-content-strategy-into-the-blend.

Bozarth, J. 2010. "Nuts and Bolts: Getting Management Support for Training." *Learning Solutions* blog, July 6. www.learningsolutionsmag.com/articles/484/nuts-and -bolts-getting-management-support-for-training.

Pollock, R., and A. Jefferson. 2012. "Ensuring Learning Transfer." *Infoline*, August. Alexandria, VA: ASTD Press.

Walsh, S. 2017. "How to Bring Your Elearning Back to Life With Curated Content." Anders Pink blog, June. http://blog.anderspink.com/2017/06/how-to-bring-your -elearning-to-life-with-curated-content.

5

Transferring Learning and Evaluating Results: How Do You Demonstrate Success?

In This Chapter

- The importance of evaluation in blended learning
- Effective practices to plan for evaluation
- How to measure learning engagement and learning transfer
- The role of authenticity in evaluation

Evaluating blended learning events helps you make informed decisions when it's time to review, revise, and renew instructional strategies, techniques, technologies, and delivery methods. When conducted throughout the blended learning experience, evaluation can measure performance objectives, refine learning resources, and ensure that learner needs are being met. Evaluation results also provide stakeholders with the information they need to guide future planning for learning solutions within the organization.

Designing and planning the evaluation process in advance will guide the development of learning resources. It will ensure that learners are satisfied with the delivered curriculum, determine what they have learned, and let you know if they were able to apply the skills they obtained.

This chapter will dive into considerations to keep in mind when evaluating blended learning, what you need to plan before evaluating, and how you can ensure you're measuring engagement with each different piece of the blended campaign.

PRO TIP

To ensure success, the evaluation plan should:
- Allow learners to self-evaluate the effectiveness of the blended learning campaign.
- Measure how well the blended learning campaign has met learning objectives and overall learning goals.
- Demonstrate the benefits of the blended learning campaign to organization stakeholders.

Evaluation and Blended Learning

Blended learning campaigns are designed to provide learners with the opportunity to master or complete learning objectives. When it comes time to assess these programs, many will simply assess the program against the individual objectives, without considering the business requirements that drove the learning objective treatment in the first place.

Any training evaluation has two goals:
- to measure if the learners have met the stated learning objectives
- to determine if meeting those learning objectives accomplished the organizational objective for which the training initiative was designed and implemented.

Evaluating blended learning campaigns introduces challenges that don't exist when evaluating traditionally delivered programs: Each content block has its own unique characteristics, whether it's a different medium or delivery technology. And it can take weeks or months to complete the formal campaign.

In a culture that relies so heavily on Level 1 reaction data (did the learners like the training, the facilitator, and the environment?), evaluating blended learning campaigns can seem daunting. But it doesn't have to be. The power and flexibility of the blended learning solution extends to evaluation as well. Because of the discrete content blocks, and the resources that are designed to be used long after the formal campaign is complete, you can collect data that are more usable and valuable to the evaluation of the program.

Consider the content block below, which is part of a larger campaign focused on teaching employees how to underwrite an insurance policy.

How to Underwrite an Insurance Policy

Lesson: Identify potential red flags when underwriting a new policy.

Instructional strategy: Case-based learning.

Instructional techniques: Moderated discussions and case studies.

Primary instructional technology: Delivered through virtual classroom.

Supporting resources:

  » Job aid (10 Critical Questions to Ask When Underwriting a New Policy)

  » Five-minute interactive e-learning session that provides a high-level illustration of the importance of uncovering this information.

Activity: After reviewing the case study, learners individually complete the job aid and then work in breakout rooms in pairs to critique each other's work.

If this lesson were delivered in a traditional format, you might collect attendance data and Level 1 reaction data. However, these two data points would not indicate if the training met its learning objectives or the business requirements—they simply tell you if people showed up and liked the experience. In addition, because the feedback is directed at the entire curriculum, there isn't any specific feedback on individual job aids and other resources. So, the data are interesting but not necessarily actionable. Generally, reaction data aren't informative enough to make changes to the design.

In a blended learning format, you can collect actionable measurements that demonstrate the impact of the project. For example, in the underwriting lesson you can track how often learners refer to the job aid and e-learning content after the formal learning ends, when learners are in the process of applying what they have learned. They can also give you feedback if any information was missing, so you can continuously update the resource, and therefore update the blended learning campaign as a whole. (This is the part of the process where your learning management system becomes critical, if you have one. To collect useful data, it helps to have a system that measures what you want measured.)

Evaluating blended learning means you are continually measuring individual resources more than you are evaluating an entire campaign, because individual lessons and their supporting resources can be packaged in the LMS and accessed by nonenrolled learners. Those are valuable data! As enrolled learners start to spread the word about how valuable individual resources are, and others start to use them, the organization will start to embrace the concept of a pull learning culture. Soon, the talent development function will be partnering with the learners and supporting ongoing business requirements.

So, yes, evaluating a blend is different.

The key to understanding the difference is in the varied learning environment and capabilities at your command in a blended learning campaign. Instead of relying on just one delivery method (for example, a classroom), you have many different technologies and environments to assess. In addition, you can draw from outside data sources—for example, misfilings in the mobile application or user latency in filing out electronic forms—to determine learner progress in meeting learning objectives. The blended learning evaluation plan can and should be more authentic and relate more to real-world performance than a traditional evaluation (such as a multiple-choice questionnaire) provides.

Take the time to inventory your process, ensure your practices are effective and followed, and remember to apply evaluation to more than learning outcomes. Did you make sure that you addressed the following?

- Instructional goals are established and communicated, including clear definitions of what will be taught and why it will be taught within a blended solution.
- A needs analysis is conducted to determine if a blended learning approach is appropriate.

- Measurable performance objectives are developed to support learner success.
- Instructional strategies, techniques, and technologies are selected in alignment with performance objectives.
- Methods for assessing learner mastery are designed in alignment with performance objectives.
- Content that supports knowledge-based objectives is designed to be delivered through self-directed technologies.
- Live learning events are designed to encourage participants to collaborate, solve problems, answer questions, and pose solutions, not to support long lectures.
- A course map is created to illustrate the balance of learning elements within the blended curriculum.
- Communication channels and tools are designed to support learner progress and reporting throughout the blended learning schedule.
- An evaluation plan is in place to determine the effectiveness of the blended learning solution.

TOOL

Evaluate your process using the practice tools found at the end of this chapter:
- "The Blended Learning Instructional Design Effective Practice Scorecard" includes the effective practice scoring tool, which lists the effective practices and provides general guidance on your score, and the effective practice scoring matrix, which assists in numerically scoring each effective practice.
- "The Effective Practice Descriptions and Recommendations" tool further describes each effective practice and provides recommendations on how to model exemplary practice in the design, development, and delivery of blended learning.

Planning to Evaluate

Before you develop evaluations for blended learning, it is critical to step back and ask some questions. The evaluation process is all about asking the right questions so you can collect the right data. Here are some to get started:

- What does success look like?
- When does measurement need to take place?

- What data should you collect?
- Who are you measuring?

Now, let's explore each of these questions, potential answers, and the process to get to those answers.

What Does Success Look Like?

The first question that absolutely must be asked and answered before creating your evaluation plan is, "What does success look like, and how will I recognize it when it happens?" To answer it, you need to go back to your needs assessment, which uncovered the needs of the organization, the gaps between current and desired performance, and what learners already know about the topic. If you haven't thoroughly documented this information, you can't identify what you want to evaluate and you're missing the baseline against which you can measure a change in learner behavior. As you look at your needs assessment, you should identify the organization's intent in delivering the blended learning campaign and the learner's intent when participating in the learning campaign. When these are aligned, you have a much better chance of selecting the appropriate behaviors to measure.

Remember, "success" should be quantifiable. You should be able to objectively measure it. For example:

- Increase overall accuracy on claim payments from 88 percent to 94 percent.
- New hires in the sales organization can be self-sufficient in seven weeks instead of 10.
- Reduce calls to the help desk on noncritical issues by 10 percent.
- Overall satisfaction with customer service is 4.5 on a 5-point scale.

You should design the overall evaluation campaign to measure these quantifiable goals.

When Should Measurement Take Place?

A fundamental characteristic of blended learning is that it is delivered over a period of weeks or months. A typical training program is evaluated at its conclusion using some postdelivery assessment. However, waiting until the end of the blended learning program for evaluation to take place means that:

- There is no opportunity to fix or improve the experience for the current learner cohort.
- If learner cohorts overlap, which is common, waiting until the end of the first cohort to evaluate the program will negatively affect multiple groups.

- Blended learning campaigns are long and there is often an extended period of time between content blocks; it is unreasonable to ask learners to evaluate an experience that may have happened weeks or months before.

It is more effective to collect feedback throughout the delivery. Evaluating each content block helps in the following ways:

- Learners get feedback about how they are performing against the desired learning objectives while they're in the training, and you can look for opportunities to close any gaps they identify.
- Program stakeholders evaluate the success (or not) of the campaign earlier in the process.
- Campaign designers can identify potential problems, whether they be instructional or technical, early enough in the program they can be addressed for the current cohort.

Think about that. The current group of learners, the individuals who identified gaps in the design, can immediately benefit if they are given the opportunity to provide feedback along the way. Often, knowledge gaps can be filled with a piece of micro-learning that you can quickly create and pilot with the group. If there are problems with activity design and learning transfer, you can address them for the next group.

Always remember that the resources in a blended learning campaign can and should be designed to be used well after the formal campaign is over. Learners should be able to access job aids, worksheets, videos, recordings, and other resources when they are applying what they've learned and when things go wrong. By collecting data about how individuals not currently enrolled in the blended learning campaign use these resources, you'll start to recognize what types of resources are most valuable. Then you can focus on these resource types in future campaigns.

Another advantage of measuring resource use outside the formal learning campaign is that you can identify the specific parts of a process that are most difficult for learners to internalize, and examine ways to streamline that process or improve the learning resources.

What Data Should You Collect?

A training program is usually in place because of an operational mandate, a regulatory requirement, a demand from the learner population, or some other external stimulus on your organization. Think about data collection from that perspective. For example, can you quantitatively answer the question, "Did you satisfy the requirement that prompted training in the first place?"

You might think that the data collection process will be too expensive, difficult, or time consuming. If your needs assessment shows that you have a training requirement, why do you need to go through this? Because even modest attempts at using simple correlations of data with other readily available information can have profound effects on your training delivery methods.

The key to using data is figuring out which data are relevant to the desired outcomes of the program, and then folding in those data as part of your evaluation plan before you deliver the training. In practice, much of the data may be readily available, but some of it might be impossible to obtain due to internal policy, regulation, or privacy. When data are available, you need to ask if it is worth collecting and directly correlates to the desired performance outcome of the blended learning campaign. My advice is to focus on the data that can be collected easily. Most organizations don't have the capacity for very complex statistical analysis of every data point, and even if they did, it is unlikely to be worth the effort to go through that process. Consider the following hypothetical questions about data collection for a blended learning program:

- Is 100 percent attendance required in a program that has eight virtual lessons as part of its blend? Why?
- Is full completion of an e-learning module important? What does it tell you?
- Is it valuable to know how often a resource like an infographic or job aid was accessed six or 12 months after the formal campaign is concluded? What will you do with that information?

If you asked these questions for several different blended learning campaigns, you would probably get a separate set of responses for each. So how much is enough? If you can ensure that the blend is meeting the business requirements and learning objectives, you are collecting enough information.

PRO TIP

Pay attention to how learners decide to participate in a blend. Are supervisors using the microlearning elements, but not participating in activities or live lessons? Are line workers fully engaged in live lessons? Are support staff only accessing introductory materials? These data show how individuals are designing personal learning pathways that meet their own needs. Not everyone needs the same depth of knowledge, and by allowing individuals to define their own learning pathways, you are making the best use of the scarcest resource you have: time.

Look for opportunities in your blended learning campaign to collect meaningful data. Consider the following content block example.

> ## How to Reduce Errors in Manufacturing
>
> **Lesson:** Reduce errors in a manufacturing process.
>
> **Instructional strategy:** Task-based learning.
>
> **Instructional techniques:** Lecture.
>
> **Primary instructional technology:** Delivered using a virtual classroom.
>
> **Supporting resources:**
>
> » job aid (Checklist to Eliminate Errors).
>
> **Activity:** Group discussion of the types of potential errors and the safety, productivity, and financial impacts of those errors.

Within this blended learning campaign, learners can enroll in the content block, or find the job aid within the learning management system without formally being part of a cohort. You can then collect data on:

- who attended the live instruction and then used the job aid
- who downloaded the job aid from the LMS, but did not attend the live instruction
- who did not attend the live instruction or access the job aid through the learning management systems.

By examining these data, you may be able to draw conclusions about the use of live instruction. Did attending the virtual classroom lesson result in a lower error rate than individuals who access the job aid without instruction, or individuals who did not access the job aid or attend the live instruction?

Perhaps the error rate doesn't change for any of the groups; this would point to a problem with the results of the needs analysis or the campaign design. For example, you may discover that the observed errors in the manufacturing process were not caused by a lack of training, but rather because of a faulty process. Or the job aid and supporting instruction were not designed in a way that closed the identified performance gap. Or closing the performance gap required a different instructional strategy, such as a project-based learning strategy that included simulations to provide practice in a more authentic learning environment (such as a laboratory or the manufacturing floor).

To make your findings more useful, you can add a data point about the job experience of the learner groups. You may decide that individuals new to the position require the live instruction and the job aid, while more experienced workers may benefit from the job aid without live instruction, perhaps supported by a short video with key points.

PRO TIP

Different learning populations don't necessarily require the same depth of instruction, and may self-select different learning pathways. Collecting observable data for each content block will help you formalize learning pathways as you revise your blended learning campaign. These data will also inform future campaigns as you start to recognize which learner groups need which types of instruction, depending on the workflow.

Who Are You Measuring?

To a large extent, the evaluation plan should focus on the design of the blended learning campaign, and whether the campaign is meeting the needs of the business and the learner. However, you should also give some thought to evaluating the people—such as the facilitator, producer, and learners—involved in the delivery of the blended learning campaign. (Be cautious in this process, however, as it can be difficult to separate the effectiveness of the people from the effectiveness of the campaign design.)

The Facilitator

When evaluating the facilitator of a blended learning campaign, focus less on the likability of the individual and more on the effectiveness to engage the learner and ensure learning is transferred. For example, say a facilitator scores a 3.5 out of 5 in the Level 1 reaction survey, but the learners in that cohort achieve a 94 percent pass rate on their final project or exam. Conversely, say a facilitator scores a 4.8 on that same scale, but the learners score below a 90 percent pass rate. How would you compare the two facilitators? Instead of looking at scores from individual cohorts, look at scores over time and see if there is a correlation between reaction data and performance outcomes.

Consider collecting the following evaluation information:

- To what extent was the facilitator present in all aspects of the blended learning campaign, not just live lessons?
- Did the facilitator exhibit behaviors that demonstrated they were comfortable communicating in nontraditional formats?
- Did the facilitator appear to support nontraditional delivery methodologies for training?

Remember, the facilitator of a blended learning campaign is more than the content expert. The facilitator has to guide the learners through instructionally complex learning paths to ensure that they stay engaged throughout the process.

The Producer

The role of the producer is evolving. In a blended learning campaign, the producer is the advocate for the learner experience and allows the facilitator to stay focused on learning and engagement. The producer focuses on helping the learners navigate technologies and meet their requirements.

Consider collecting the following evaluation information:

- To what extent did the producer advocate for the learners? For example, were struggling learners identified and supported?
- To what extent were technical and logistical questions answered in a timely manner, and how easy were the answers to follow?
- To what extent did the producer exhibit proficiency in managing and answering questions about instructional technologies?
- Did the producer exhibit behaviors that demonstrated they were comfortable communicating in nontraditional formats?

Use your evaluation results to help determine where the producer can best add value to the process, and tighten up the job description so all future blended learning campaigns can be more successful.

Typically, the learner provides the feedback about the facilitator and the producer; you should include several checkpoints in a longer blended learning campaign so there is opportunity to improve the experience if a problem is identified.

Use the same evaluations to improve the partnership between the facilitator and the producer. The facilitation team should schedule multiple checkpoints where they can share constructive feedback and discuss their perceptions of the effectiveness of the campaign to date.

The Learner

Learner assessments can be integrated with an evaluation of the blended learning campaign to provide insight to learner progress and the achievement of organizational and personal outcomes.

Consider collecting the following evaluation information:

- To what extent did the learner participate in all the aspects of the blended learning campaign, including live sessions, social collaborative activities, e-learning, and microlearning?
- How did the learner perform on assessments, and how did that performance compare with others with equivalent participation?
- What conclusions can you draw when you compare participation rates and assessment results?

It can be tempting to assume that a nonparticipative learner is a "bad" learner. But be careful of jumping to those conclusions. Always measure against desired performance outcomes and business requirements to draw your correlations.

TOOL

Delivering or participating in blended learning campaigns requires individuals to develop new skills. It is important to measure these skills to continuously improve the experience and move the organization along the change curve. The "Learner Evaluation Worksheet" tool at the end of this chapter allows learners to evaluate the success of facilitator, producer, and themselves in the blended learning campaign.

Measuring Learner Engagement and Learning Transfer

Because blended learning programs last longer than a traditional one- or two-day workshop, it's difficult to maintain momentum and interest in the content. Learner engagement is critical to the success of your campaign, so it's an important factor to consider as part of your evaluation plan.

That said, engagement can be difficult to quantify and even define regarding training programs. Charles Dye (2016), lead researcher at my company, InSync Training, defines learner engagement based on three factors:

- **Emotion:** How does the learner feel about the content and its presentation or treatment?
- **Intellect:** Does the instructional experience require and involve the learner's intellect?
- **Environment:** Do the learners interact with the learning environment and is the environment changed because of the training?

Measuring Engagement

As with design, development, and implementation, measuring engagement in a blended learning campaign adds its own level of complexity. We have to evaluate whether our programs met the learning objectives, improved performance, and supported learners' professional development. This is especially challenging given the number of informal moments of learning that blended learning includes.

I've found Charles Dye's guidance on measuring learner engagement to be immensely helpful. In his article, "Learner Engagement: Why It Is Important," Dye says to remember:

- **It's dynamic.** Learners engage at different rates and levels throughout a single blended learning campaign. Understanding that changes happen on a moment-to-moment basis helps us compartmentalize engagement at each stage of the learning process.
- **Behavioral change provides a starting point for measurement.** Learners' intellectual reaction to content or subject matter often affects their behavior change within a learning environment. Closely observe your learners' behavior during formal events to gauge initial reactions to the program. Adjust accordingly, if possible.
- **Learners have preconceptions about learning,** which influence their engagement in programs for both better and worse. For example, a new supervisor is uncomfortable giving feedback, you can assume that conducting a performance review will be difficult. You can assist them by providing additional activities and solutions to help them bridge the feedback gap. The flexibility of blended learning

TOOL

How do you measure engagement? Use the "Measuring Learner Engagement in a Blended Learning Environment" tool at the end of this chapter to get started.

allows this to happen using personalized learning paths. But, it takes ongoing measurement of individual learner experience and mastery to be able to determine what personalization is necessary.

- **Each treatment requires its own distinct measurement approach.** It's important to remember that we have to measure learner engagement in every learning environment we include in our blended programs. Just as we select authentic design treatments for each learning objective, we must also select appropriate measurement tools and approaches for each treatment. For example, learner performance in an online self-paced simulation can provide data such as how long it takes to perform a task. Those data can be coupled with the number of times a learner refers to a job aid to help you determine the level of mastery for the task. Similarly, in a parallel learning environment, such as a live in-person simulation, the speed with which a learner performs also allows you to measure how long it takes to complete a task.

Incorporating engagement measurements into your instructional design methodology adds another dynamic to improve the potential success of your program and its learners. Here are a couple examples of how to measure the elusive concept of engagement in relation to blended learning.

Measuring Performance Around What Was Taught

When we think about assessment, traditional test taking comes to mind. If learners score well on a test, we assume that they understood the content and will successfully perform skills based on that content. There's comfort in data—we recognize numbers, because, fundamentally, they're measurable.

Blended learning is different because engagement influences learner behavior. Our assessment approach should take that into consideration. Charles Dye (2016) argues, "In answering the question of learner performance with respect to engagement, [we must] define measure(s) of performance, establish rubrics based on them that are situated in real-world contexts, and provide instruction in different learning environments. If the right environment with situated content is presented to the learner, the learner's engagement goes up, learner self-efficacy improves, and achievement (even that just measured by typical testing) improves."

Learning How to Learn in a Different Environment

Learning environments also affect how learners collaborate, create, and learn. In each environment, learners develop skills for navigating and managing the experience.

Ultimately, this means learners aren't just learning the content. They're also learning how to learn in each element of the blend. Dye explains, "If the learning environment is based on—or, even better, uses—a real-world context, the learner develops true competence by participating in the learning experience; the knowledge and skills developed in the instructional experience are directly transferable to the real-world task."

Measuring Learning Transfer

How will you know when a person is finished with a learning experience that largely relies on self-directed learning? Modern blended learning design assumes that informal learning, especially learning that goes on long after the formal campaign has concluded, is part of the process. Therefore, measuring learning transfer doesn't just occur during the formal event, but for as long as the learner needs to interact with the subject matter.

At first, you can make some assumptions. For example, if a learner accesses a piece of content 12 times in the first three months, and only five times in the following three months, and never again after that, you can assume that the content associated with that job aid was fully mastered in six months. But, some learners will continue to access that same job aid every time they need to perform that task. Does that mean this group of learners never mastered the task? Not necessarily.

If you can determine that the individuals who always access the job aid complete the task more quickly and accurately, you can assume that the job aid should be used every time the task is performed, and adjust process accordingly.

Remember, modern learners are learning perpetually. Talent development organizations, therefore, need to find ways to perpetually measure learning transfer.

The Role of Authenticity in Evaluation

Another advantage of the flexibility of a blended learning campaign is the ability to create authentic learning environments. The more authentic the learning environment, the more relevant the content is to the learners and the easier it is for them to map their experience in the training program to their daily work.

The content block design allows you to deliver content in the most authentic environment for that particular block. In the case of sales training, for example, content blocks concerned with researching a prospect can be delivered to the salesperson's desk, which is where that research will probably happen when real work is being performed. Teaching individuals how to research clients while in a classroom with 20 other people can work, but not as well as at their own desks with authentic resources surrounding them, such as printed materials, colleagues, and access to previously saved documents and presentations. And don't underestimate the comfort of learning in a familiar place.

How does this relate to measurement? In a classroom situation, learning professionals might design role plays and other activities that have a foregone conclusion—you put the right information in the right place for learners to access so they can learn the process. Assessment scores by a learner in this classroom situation should be very high, because you place them in a situation with immediate instructor guidance and near-guaranteed success. But are these scores truly representative of the effectiveness of your content block?

By delivering that same assessment at the individual's desk, you'll get much more realistic scores. You can even design the assessment to take advantage of a potential prospect the office is currently investigating. Learners will learn to depend on the resources they have and can go through this problem-based approach on their own.

Evaluating Your Blended Learning Campaign

Evaluation is a time-consuming and detailed-oriented process that's easy to skip or treat as an afterthought. After all, everyone is more interested in the actual training product, whether designing it or rolling it out.

However, blended learning campaigns are instructionally complex, which makes them expensive when it comes to learners' time, technology investments, development costs, and administration. The cost of not evaluating what has worked and what hasn't can be even more expensive. So, remember to evaluate along the way; don't wait for the end of a campaign to collect data. The results of each content block should be measured against the learning objective and the business requirements.

RESOURCE

See chapters 6 and 10 in in *Essentials for Blended Learning* by Jared Stein and Charles R. Graham (2014) for additional ideas on assessing and evaluating blended learning.

Here is some advice for simplifying the process:

- Write down, in your own words, what the organization wants to accomplish with the blended learning campaign based on the needs analysis. What behaviors to they want to affect? What performance indicators need to improve?

- Capture baseline data on these behaviors and performance indicators. The program sponsors, the ones who recognize there is a problem, will have these answers. For example:
    » Currently, calls are being answered on the seventh ring.
    » Error rates on the manufacturing line average 72 percent.
- Document the desired state for these behaviors and performance indicators. This is the performance gap, which will drive your learning objectives.
- Answer the following questions:
    » How will you collect these data? How often?
    » Where are the data? Who owns them?
    » How will you present the data? To whom?
    » What will you do with the data you do collect?
- If you find you are collecting data upon which you never act, stop. Data collection can be time consuming, and if you aren't using the data, it's a waste of resources.
- Look for options to automate data collection and presentation. Start with your LMS.

PRO TIP

If you use an LMS, it can automate the collection of many types of data, including:
- what content is being accessed
- what interactive content is being completed, and what the completion rates are
- how long it takes to complete tasks, and where learners struggle
- Level 1 and Level 2 evaluation results.

In addition, as LMSs become more robust, they are also collecting data about learners' experiences in collaborative forums and other social media environments.

What's Next

Training evaluation is a field unto itself. If you need to learn more about how to design specific evaluation tools or how to implement an evaluation plan, there are many tools, books, and workshops that can help you. And once you master how to evaluate the effectiveness and business impact of blended learning campaigns, you'll become a sought-after resource in your organization.

Questions to Explore

- How do you measure individuals in your training programs today? Do you act on the data appropriately? How?
- When do you measure learner success today? When do you stop?
- How do you define learner engagement? Is it something you consider in your design?
- What types of data do your organization collect now? What do you do with it? Are any data superfluous?

Tools for Support

Blended Learning Instructional Design Effective Practice Scorecard

Effective Practice Scoring Tool

Use this tool to determine how effectively you're using the following blended learning practices. Read the following descriptions and score each one. (See the scoring matrix on the next page for more guidance on how to numerically score each practice.)

Points: 0 = Lacking, 1 = Emerging, 2 = Established, 3 = Exemplary

#	Description	Points
1	Instructional goals are established and communicated, including clear definitions of what will be taught and why within a blended solution.	
2	A needs analysis is conducted to determine if a blended learning approach is appropriate for the learning program.	
3	Measurable performance objectives are developed to support learner success.	
4	Modes of delivery and technologies are selected in alignment with performance objectives.	
5	Methods and approaches for assessing learner mastery are designed in alignment with performance objectives.	
6	Learning material which supports knowledge-based objectives is designed to be delivered through self-paced technologies.	
7	Live learning events are designed to encourage participants to collaborate, solve problems, answer questions, and pose solutions.	
8	A course map is created to illustrate the balance of learning elements within the blended curriculum.	
9	Communication channels and tools are designed to support learner progress and reporting throughout the blended learning schedule.	
10	An evaluation plan is in place to determine the effectiveness of the blended learning solution.	
	Total	

Scoring

If you scored:

0-10: There's room for improvement! If you find that many of these practices are not observed or implemented in a blended learning solution, take some time to review the design approach and intentionally include these effective practices.

11-20: You're on the right track! Explore the areas which are scored low, and explore our recommendations to better integrate those effective practices into the design process.

21-30: Bravo! Your team is well on the way to designing, developing, and delivering a blended learning model of excellence. Take some time to share your success with our community.

Effective Practice Scoring Matrix

Use this matrix for guidance on how to score each practice in the scoring tool on the previous page.

Effective Practice	Emerging (1 Point)	Established (2 Points)	Exemplary (3 Points)
1. Instructional goals are established and communicated, including clear definitions of what will be taught and why.	Instructional goals are established, but there is no clear message on what will be taught, or why a blended solution is being considered.	Instructional goals are established, communicated, and shared with stakeholders.	Instructional goals are established, communicated, and shared with stakeholders. An executive summary expands on what will be taught, and why.
2. A needs analysis is conducted to determine if a blended learning approach is appropriate.	A needs analysis was done for only face-to-face or full online delivery, with no consideration for a blended solution.	A needs analysis was conducted and the learners' situation was considered.	A needs analysis was conducted and the learners' situation was considered. Results were compared to current and future instructional goals and performance objectives.

Effective Practice	Emerging (1 Point)	Established (2 Points)	Exemplary (3 Points)
3. Measurable performance objectives support learner success.	Objectives exist but are not framed to measure learner performance or success.	Measurable performance objectives are clear and achievable, and fit with the overall instructional goal.	Measurable performance objectives are clear and achievable, and fit with the overall instructional goal. Objectives are balanced, scaffolding learners from lower-order to higher-order thinking.
4. Modes of delivery and technologies are aligned with performance objectives.	Performance objectives were reviewed during the selection of technologies and delivery modes.	Performance objectives drove the consideration and selection of technologies and delivery modes.	Performance objectives drove the consideration, evaluation, and selection of technologies and delivery modes. A curriculum map illustrates the relationship between learning objectives, content, and delivery modes.
5. Methods and approaches for assessing learner mastery are aligned with performance objectives.	Performance objectives were reviewed while designing methods and approaches for assessing learner mastery.	Performance objectives drove the consideration and selection of methods and approaches to assessing learner mastery.	Performance objectives drove the consideration and selection of methods and approaches to assessing learner mastery. A curriculum map illustrates the alignment of thinking levels to assessment approaches.
6. Learning material supports knowledge-based objectives delivered through self-paced technologies.	Knowledge-based learning materials were translated into self-paced learning treatments.	Self-paced materials support knowledge-based objectives.	Self-paced materials support knowledge-based objectives, and include options for self-reflections on learning.

Effective Practice	Emerging (1 Point)	Established (2 Points)	Exemplary (3 Points)
7. Live learning events encourage learners to collaborate, solve problems, answer questions, and pose solutions.	Live learning events include participation and collaboration.	Live learning events include collaboration and support higher-order thinking levels.	Live learning events include collaboration and support higher-order thinking levels. Delivery approaches promote the instructor as facilitator, not lecturer. Promotes co-creating learning assets and reflections.
8. A course map illustrates the balance of learning elements within the blended curriculum.	A calendar or schedule of learning treatments exists.	A course map exists with an overview of the entire blended learning curriculum was created.	A course map exists with an overview of the entire blended learning curriculum. Time management tools and checklists are available.
9. Communication channels and tools support learner progress and reporting.	Tools and methods for communication and tracking progress are available.	Communication channels include feedback and reporting mechanisms to guide learners as they progress through the program.	Communication channels include feedback mechanisms to guide learners as they progress through the program. Milestones and achievements are also shared within the learning community.
10. An evaluation plan is in place to determine the effectiveness of the blended learning solution.	Learners have a method to self-evaluate the effectiveness of the blended learning solution.	An evaluation plan measures how well the blended learning solution has met performance objectives and overall learning goals.	An evaluation plan measures how well the blended learning solution has met performance objectives and overall learning goals. Evaluations to demonstrate the program's benefits to the organization's stakeholders.

Effective Practice Scorecard Descriptions and Recommendations

Use the following recommendations to learn more about how to model each exemplary practice in the design, development, and delivery of blended learning.

Effective Practice 1

Instructional goals are established and communicated, including clear definitions of what will be taught, and why it will be taught within a blended solution.

When instructional goals are established for a blended learning solution, the entire team needs to be made aware of what materials will be taught, and why the learners would benefit from a blend of delivery methodologies. Once this information is defined and communicated, the team can begin to determine the best way to design a blended solution.

Blended learning solutions are just that—a blend of the best delivery methodologies available for a specific objective. It is less about the technology available, and more about the needs and priorities of the learning community as framed within established instructional goals.

Asking "What?" and "Why?" will guide the design process and help determine which elements work best in online, classroom-based instruction, electronic performance support, paper-based, and formalized or informal on-the-job solutions.

Recommendations:
- Clearly communicate the instructional goals of the learning solution.
- Remember to ask "why" along with "what."
- If this is your first blended learning instructional design project, reframe the needs analysis to focus on the "why" to better inform your design.
- Create an executive summary which expands on what will be taught, and why it will be taught within a blended solution.
- Ask for feedback on the summary from key stakeholders to be sure that you are on track.
- Share the summary and feedback with your learning designers, developers, facilitators, and producers.

Effective Practice 2

A needs analysis is conducted to determine if a blended learning approach is appropriate for the learning program.

The needs analysis phase is critical to the design, development, and delivery of learning solutions, and it will benefit the entire learning team (and learners) to consider if a blended approach is appropriate.

Needs analyses are tied closely to instructional goals, as well as organizational goals. As you craft your needs analysis, consider what solutions have been effective in the past, and do research to find out, as best you can, where the organization as a whole is headed.

If the results tell you that a blended learning solution is not the right fit, consider going back to the instructional goal and ask the "what" and "why" questions again.

Recommendations:

- Review past, current, and future instructional approaches before you conduct a needs analysis.
- Consider how, where, and when people work and learn.
- Refer back to the "what" and "why" of the instructional goals before you conduct your needs analysis.
- Compare results to current and future instructional goals and performance objectives.

Effective Practice 3

Measurable performance objectives are developed to support learner success.

Performance objectives indicate what learners will be able to do at the end of the training. Taking the time to craft meaningful performance objectives will guide learner success and ensure that the blended learning solution will support the overall instructional goals.

Focus on the audience, behavior, condition, and criteria for success when creating learner-centered objectives.

To create measurable performance objectives:

1. Identify the learner.
2. Describe what the learner will be able to do when learning is complete.
3. Specify the conditions under which the performance is to occur.
4. Detail the criteria used to evaluate learner performance.

Measurable performance objectives provide a road map to the design of a successful blended learning program. They provide guidelines on how to assess learning, and establish the pathway for participants to explore throughout their learning journey.

Recommendations:
- Review your learning objectives as a whole to be sure that they create a learning pathway.
- If applicable, create objectives that guide the scaffolding of learning from lower-order to higher-order thinking.
- If you are converting to a blend from a face-to-face environment, take this opportunity to review your performance objectives to ensure that they are still applicable within the blended solution.
- Explore the Writing Measurable Objectives job aid in the InSync Blended Learning Hub.

Effective Practice 4

Modes of delivery and technologies are selected in alignment with performance objectives.

Performance objectives should drive the consideration, evaluation, and selection of technologies and delivery modes. Once you identify the performance objectives, you should decide how you will know whether or not a participant has mastered each objective.

Following these simple steps can help guide your selection of delivery modes throughout the blended learning design process:

1. Determine what needs to be taught, and what associated objectives are included in that topic.
2. Establish if the associated objectives can be assessed online. If they can be assessed online, the associated learning can be taught online.
3. Decide whether or not collaboration would enhance learning associated with the objective by asking these questions:
   - » Is there a purpose to bringing learners together?
   - » Does mastery of this objective require the synergy of a group?
   - » Will the outcome for participants be better because we have brought them together to learn?

By taking the time to step through this process, you can design a blended learning strategy that combines virtual classes, face-to-face classes, and independent work, that best achieves your performance objectives.

Recommendations:

- Take the time to review each individual learning event and all associated performance objectives before you begin a conversation about delivery modes.
- Create a curriculum map to illustrate the relationship between learning objectives, learning content, and selected modes of delivery.
- Refer to the Blended Learning Decision Making Flow Diagram when exploring technologies and modes of delivery.

Effective Practice 5

Methods and approaches for assessing learner mastery are designed in alignment with performance objectives.

Blended learning is not only about matching content to the most appropriate delivery medium, but doing it at the learning objective level. It's the assessment technique that marries these two concepts.

Learning activities and assessments should be designed to support the mastery of performance objectives. Activity and assessment types are typically discussed and designed alongside the delivery mode review process.

As there is generally a direct correlation between the type of assessment you will use and the type of technology you will use, it is important to loop back to the performance objectives on a regular basis to be sure that your design stays on target with learner success always in mind.

Recommendations:

- List all performance objectives associated with each activity and assessment to be sure that all objectives will be achievable.
- If scaffolded learning is part of the instructional goal, create a curriculum map to illustrate the alignment of lower- and higher-order thinking levels to assessment approaches.
- Loop back through the delivery mode selection process to be sure that the delivery modes selected are appropriate for each activity and assignment.

Effective Practice 6

Learning material that supports knowledge-based objectives is designed to be delivered through self-paced technologies.

Knowledge-based objectives, such as remembering and understanding, are well suited for self-paced learning. Learning objectives that use keywords such as "recognize," "list," "identify," "define," and "locate" fit within that scope.

When designing blended learning solutions, consider technologies that focus on disseminating information, with little or no connection or collaboration with other learners (or the instructor) required.

Recommendations:

- Focus on the design of interactions between learners and content for knowledge-based objectives.
- Ensure that participants have detailed instructions on how to access and complete all self-paced materials.
- Provide opportunities for learners to reflect on or share their self-paced learning experiences within the blended learning solution.

Effective Practice 7

Live learning events are designed to encourage participants to collaborate, solve problems, answer questions, and pose solutions.

The time set aside for live events in any blended learning solution should focus on collaboration, not on information dissemination. Real-time events (face-to-face or virtual) can be designed to review key concepts, provide feedback, and create the opportunity to work in groups to solve a learning challenge.

Loop back to the blended learning delivery mode selection process, where we asked if collaboration would enhance learning associated with the performance objectives. The live events are where we establish the purpose for bringing learners together, harness the synergy of the group, and achieve better outcomes based on input from and interaction among learning peers.

Recommendations:

- Delivery approaches should be designed to promote the instructor as facilitator, not lecturer, within all live learning events.
- Provide and promote options for co-creating and sharing learning assets.
- Provide opportunities for learners to reflect on or share their live learning experiences within the blended learning solution.

Effective Practice 8

A course map is created to illustrate the balance of learning elements within the blended curriculum.

The course map provides an overview of the entire blended learning curriculum by explaining the sequence of events, the types of learning activities, the anticipated length for each activity, and an indication of when the activity will take place.

Course maps provide details of the journey for learners, helping them to get started, find their learning pathway, and determine what it will take to complete the journey.

While the map details the phases of the learning journey for the learner, it also provides an overview of the balance within the blended learning solution for the designer. Reviewing the course map will enable designers to better determine if there is a correct balance and application of content, interaction, and assessment modes within the blend.

Recommendations:
- Create a checklist to go along with the course map to help guide participants on their learning journey.
- Include time management tips and tools (or link to them) within the course map.
- Integrate the course map into every learning event within the blended learning solution to be sure that learners know how they are progressing within their learning journey.

Effective Practice 9

Communication channels and tools are designed to support learner progress and reporting throughout the blended learning schedule.

Communication channels allow instructors and learners to connect and collaborate within the blended learning environment. As learners work on their own or in groups, these communication channels provide value by enabling the exchange of information and ideas, as well as the creation of new knowledge.

Communication channels provide a means for instructors to keep learners on track, and for learners to report on their progress. These channels need to serve a purpose, and be associated with performance objectives. This association will ensure that participants keep progressing, learning, and sharing.

Recommendations:

- When creating a communication channel, remember to focus on the associated learning objectives.
- Design communication channels to include feedback mechanisms to guide learners as they progress through the learning curriculum.
- Provide a means within the channel to communicate milestones and achievements within the learning community.

Effective Practice 10

An evaluation plan is in place to determine the effectiveness of the blended learning solution.

Evaluation of all learning events leads to informed decisions to review, revise, and renew materials and modes of delivery. Conducted throughout the blended learning experience, evaluation can help better define performance objectives, refine learning materials, and ensure that learner needs are being met.

Designing and planning the evaluation process in advance will guide the development of learning materials and blended delivery methods. It will ensure that learners are satisfied with the delivered curriculum, determine that they have learned, and let you know if they are able to apply the skills they have obtained.

Evaluation results also provide stakeholders with information to guide future planning for learning solutions within the organization.

Recommendations:

- Clearly state (and continuously refine) the purpose of conducting any evaluation in advance.
- Share the purpose of the evaluation along with the results.
- Ask for feedback from stakeholders, and continuously refine your evaluation methods.

Learner Evaluation Worksheet

Evaluating the human part of blended learning is as important as evaluating the content design. If the people aren't actively supporting the process, the program will struggle to move forward.

Encourage learners to evaluate the facilitator, producer, and themselves. Avoid asking too many questions—learners can suffer from evaluation fatigue. Only ask the questions on which you can act.

Questions for learner evaluation of the facilitator:

- To what extent was the facilitator present in all aspects of the blended learning campaign, not just in the live lessons? For example, did the facilitator participate in discussion boards and email communications?
- Did the facilitator exhibit behaviors that demonstrated they were comfortable communicating in nontraditional formats? For example, did they only facilitate in a lecture style?
- Did the facilitator appear to support nontraditional delivery methodologies for training?
- How could the facilitator have made your personal learning journey more effective or productive?

Questions for learner evaluation of the producer:

- To what extent did the producer advocate for you as a learner? For example, if you were struggling with content or technology, did the producer proactively support you?
- To what extent were technical and logistical questions answered in a timely manner, and how easy to follow where the answers?
- To what extent did the producer exhibit proficiency with managing and answering questions about any instructional technologies?
- Did the producer exhibit behaviors that demonstrated they were comfortable communicating in nontraditional formats?
- How could the producer have made your personal learning journey more effective or productive?

Questions for learner self-reflection:

- Did you commit to the learning campaign and complete what you needed to achieve your desired level of mastery?
- Did you prioritize your learning, scheduling time for self-directed activities and lessons, or did you wait until the last minute to complete, if at all?
- Did you participate fully in live lessons and social collaborative forums, such as discussions boards?
- What would your peers say about your participation and contributions in the program? Have you earned a place in their personal learning networks?
- How could you have made your personal learning journey more effective or productive?

Measuring Learner Engagement in a Blended Learning Environment

Learner engagement should alway be a priority for your blended learning programs. However, tracking and measuring this engagement across the blend isn't always easy. Consider using this post-delivery instrument as part of your measurement plan. Administer this survey immediately following the delivery of your program, and look for response data trends along the three factors of engagement:

- **Cognitive:** What did the leaner think about the instructional experience?
- **Environmental:** Was the learner situated in an environment where the training was effectively delivered?
- **Affective:** How did the learner feel about the instructional experience?

Look for evidence to make modest changes to your implementation based on the data, by looking for trends indicating that the blended program achieved its objectives in a meaningful environment, or simply made participants feel good about the topic.

Check the most appropriate level of agreement (1 = strongly disagree; 5 = strongly agree).

	Disagree				Agree
Cognitive	1	2	3	4	5
• The instructional program was important for my personal or professional development.	□	□	□	□	□
• I learned something new in the subject area from the instructor.	□	□	□	□	□
• The materials and concepts presented in the instructional program were well suited to my level of expertise.	□	□	□	□	□
Environmental					
• The materials, activities, and references provided me everything I needed to perform well in the instructional program.	□	□	□	□	□
• I was comfortable with the method of instructional treatment and delivery.	□	□	□	□	□
• I was able to participate effectively in the instructional delivery.	□	□	□	□	□
Affective					
• The subject matter in the instructional program was important to me.	□	□	□	□	□
• I felt good about participating in the discussions and activities of the instructional program.	□	□	□	□	□
• I felt encouraged to volunteer my opinion in the instructional program.	□	□	□	□	□
• The instructor presented the learning content in ways that helped me to learn.	□	□	□	□	□

Used with permission from Dye (2016).

Additional Resources

Bersin, J. 2015. *The Blended Learning Book: Best Practices, Proven Methodologies, and Lessons Learned,* 2nd Edition. San Francisco: Pfeiffer.

Dye, C. 2016. "Virtually There: Learner Engagement—Why is it Important?" InSync Training blog, May 12. http://blog.insynctraining.com/virtually -there-learner-engagement-why-is-it-important.

Stein, J., and C.R. Graham. 2014. *Essentials for Blended Learning: A Standards-Based Guide.* New York: Routledge.

6

Planning Next Steps: Where Do You Go From Here?

In This Chapter

- Why blended learning is more critical than ever
- Tips to ensure the ongoing success of your program
- The future of blended learning
- How to design your personal blended learning campaign

One of the most common realizations learning professionals have as they evolve into learning experience architects is that blended learning design and implementation is much more complex than they anticipated.

A colleague once summed it up succinctly. She said that, when designing for a blended learning solution, you need to think about a much more complex choreography than you would for a traditional face-to-face solution. You need to consider how to integrate learners, facilitators, producers, and technology throughout the process. Every participant in this "dance" might be doing something independently, but the outcome needs to be a synchronized flow of information.

As mentioned in chapter 1, it's a four-dimensional problem. The key to blended learning design is ensuring that the right content is in the right place at the right time, and delivered to the right audience of learners.

- **The right content:** When we discuss having the right content, it means a rigorous application of instructional design. Due to the instructional complexity of the blended learning campaign, consisting of multiple instructional strategies, techniques, and technologies, rushing through the design process at any point could readily result in a failure. Instructional design is indeed more critical than ever before. And, when we fail to apply the required rigor, our learners will often disengage from the blend before we realize there's a problem.

- **The right place:** Delivering content to the right place really addresses the concept of authenticity. Modern learners can engage in pieces of the blend from traditional classrooms, at their desks, on their mobile devices while away from traditional work settings, and on the job. The challenge for a learning experience architect is to anticipate where the learner might be applying the content after the formal training is over, and deliver that content to the most authentic environment.

- **The right time:** Traditionally, learning organizations have excelled at anticipating and supporting when learners need to acquire new skills. But modern blended learning design needs to address every moment of learning need, including applying what they've learned back on the job, and supporting the learner when things go wrong. By supporting these moments of learning need, you ensure that you are partnering with the learners to meet business requirements.

- **The right audience:** Blended learning design is not a one-size-fits-all recipe. The flexibility of content block design—each block having its own lessons, activities, and assessments—allows the learning experience architect to develop and evolve unique learning paths for different learning personas based on their individual needs.

RESOURCE

In May 2017, the Pew Research Center produced a report titled *The Future of Jobs and Job Training* (Rainie and Anderson 2017). Chock-full of useful insights and expert advice, it tackles five major themes about the future of jobs training in the technology age. Consult it for thoughts on how you might prepare as training shifts to a more hybrid, blended learning model.

The modern business landscape, with its focus on mobility, collaboration, and globalization, requires you to continue to evolve learning design and become fluent in a language that is not focused on delivery methodologies like webinars and e-learning; it is focused on the type of event in which a learner is participating, like a lesson, activity, or assessment.

Getting the right content to the right place at the right time for the right audience will help you meet the needs of the business. But you also need to meet the needs of your learners. As discussed in chapter 2, modern learners are overworked, overwhelmed, and constantly distracted. They have very distinct needs when it comes to how they learn, requiring more than planned, formal training initiatives; they also require the ability to get content when they need it. If it is not provided by the internal talent development department, or if the content isn't easily accessible, they will resort to other unvetted ways of getting what they need, like using search engines.

What Makes a Blend Special?

If you have started to design a blended learning campaign, or are in the process of implementing a campaign, you already understand that this is a complex process. Planning and development require a lot of time and resources, and maintaining learner engagement throughout this longer learning process requires concentrated attention from the implementation team.

But you probably also realize that the time and resources spent really pay off at the end. A well-designed blended learning campaign is powerful in its flexibility, its ability to time-release learning content, and its capacity to meet the needs of the business.

- **Flexibility.** The flexibility of a blend comes in the ability to create discrete content resources that can support formal lessons and informal moments of learner need. These resources and lessons can be arranged to create learning paths that meet the needs of different individuals and learner audiences. And, if something changes, an individual resource can be updated without having a large impact on the rest of the design.

- **Time-released learning.** Traditionally, training initiatives have been compressed into tight packages of time. When delivered in a classroom, this approach was economical because learners did not need to leave their desks and their workflow multiple times, which would have been disruptive and costly. Today's learning landscape allows us to deliver content over a period of time that makes sense. We can identify how much time is required for a learner to absorb and reflect upon the new content or skills delivered in each individual lesson, and begin the next lesson after the appropriate period of time has passed. We're no longer teaching a salesperson how to make a sales presentation on their second day on the job. Rather, we deliver that lesson closer to the time we expect that they will make a sales presentation.

- **Meeting business requirements.** Ultimately, any learning campaign needs to meet the needs of the business. We do need to be able to measure against the requirements outlined during the needs assessment. Blended learning design's flexible approach allows us to not just meet the requirements of the business, but also to show that we're meeting those needs even after the formal campaign is concluded. And when new gaps are identified, or improvement is needed, individual resources and lessons can be updated relatively quickly to close those gaps.

So, what makes a blend special? When we expand our definition of modern blended learning to include not just the formal campaign, but the learning that happens in each moment of learning need, we start to see how blended learning helps us meet the needs of our overwhelmed, overworked, and distracted modern learners.

It reinforces the modern workplace learning mindset shared in chapter 2. All learning is valuable, and learning happens without your intervention. Your job is to ensure learners have the tools they need when they need them, and the foundation to use those tools well.

This is a change. To manage the change to modern blended learning, which is (or soon will be) all learning, you need to manage the change by partnering with both your learners and your business.

Instructional Design Is More Critical Than Ever

For years, there has been discussion around whether traditional instructional design has a role in the modern learning landscape. Chapter 3 established that the process is not only still relevant but also more critical than ever. Of course, it is evolving. With that, the role of instructional designer is also evolving into a learning experience architect.

Needs assessment is more critical than ever—it's too expensive and time consuming to create the wrong training. In a pull learning environment, modern learners will quickly dismiss content they decide is irrelevant, sloppy, or incorrect. It can be very difficult for talent development to recover from this loss of trust.

To remain relevant into the future, practitioners need to design learning campaigns instead of courses, and keep up to date on the latest instructional strategies, techniques, and technologies. Content should be able to stand on its own, so when pulled by a learner the objective stays in context. It also needs to be able to be integrated, so all the resources can be arranged into specific learning paths depending on the needs of the individual.

This takes skill and expertise. More than ever before, advanced instructional design skills are what will make the learning experience successful for all stakeholders.

Ensuring Ongoing Success

The key to ensure your blended learning experiences are met with success is to make the process repeatable. Constantly review and update your planning worksheets and checklists to ensure that they're accurate. Capture comments in the moment as to what assumptions you made that did or did not work, and recommendations for the next implementation. Each individual campaign should be a case study for colleagues in the learning organization, and a template for the next blended learning campaign.

Establish a Review and Evaluation Cycle

The evaluation process discussed in chapter 5 should add value beyond an individual campaign. The results of ongoing evaluation should inform and help you design future blended learning campaigns. Establishing a review and evaluation cycle should be part of the instructional strategy within a blended learning design implementation. As you frame out each phase of the design, development, and delivery stages, build in time for reflection and feedback.

When you create your evaluation plan, start by asking yourself, "What does success look like and how will I recognize it when it happens?" As your organization implements blended learning campaigns, the answer to this question will become better defined. Use past evaluation results to improve the learner experience, make design decisions, and avoid repeating past mistakes. (See the reflection tool in chapter 1 to facilitate the evaluation of your blended learning efforts.)

Examples and approaches include:

- Formalize and assign a team member to the role of planning worksheet or checklist coordinator. Host a quarterly review meeting to discuss how teams are using these resources and what changes need to be made. This is an excellent role for someone new to the team who needs to learn more about the processes and strategies involved in the design, development, delivery, and management of blended learning.

- Create a simple one-page case study template that includes a brief description of the objective and solution and lists three or four bullet points related to process and results for each. These are easy to update and can be used as a reference for marketing and stakeholder buy-in, and to guide the design of future projects.

- Create feedback channels that make it easy for learners, team members, and mangers to provide their insight and opinion, and share those results across teams. All survey data and feedback should be centralized so that any team member involved in the blended learning initiative can access it. A comment from a learner who is inspired by the design of a simple infographic might shape a new marketing message to gain stakeholder buy-in.

- Develop and deliver a quarterly or annual project report, including what the objectives of the blended learning initiative were, and how well these objectives were met. Include the case studies you have created throughout each phase of the project, along with narrative impressions from each team involved in the initiative. Wrap up the report with recommendations for future iterations or new projects.

Remember, the review process requires reflection, and reflection takes time. Make it a priority to build that time into your blended learning initiative project planning schedule.

Create and Execute an Internal Marketing Plan

Within organizations, word travels fast. Make sure that the news about bended learning has a positive spin. Part of any solid modern learning implementation involves marketing the new program, promoting it to learners and stakeholders, and managing the message about the experience.

Learning professionals tend to announce new programs, and then expect learners to remember they exist. If we are adopting a perpetual learning model, the same must be true of our internal marketing. Share regular news about upcoming campaigns and learner achievements to build buzz and create a highly interested audience. Most importantly, however, ongoing program promotion can modernize your organization's learning culture.

In my experience, a successful blended learning marketing campaign highlights:

- what's in it for learners
- new and helpful blended learning resources available to learners
- the results of recent programs for individual learners and the organization at large.

A marketing plan reinforces the idea that learning, whether formal or informal, provides value, and that the training function serves to partner with learners while addressing larger business goals.

TOOL

The "Blended Learning Marketing Plan Worksheet" tool at the end of this chapter provides an opportunity to reflect on how to market your initiative to your audience.

Partner With Managers

Chapter 2 discussed partnering with the business to ensure ongoing success. Engaging managers is critical to this partnership.

When learners have the support of their managers, they're more likely to engage and take ownership of their learning pathways within blended programs. In addition to hosting an introductory session for managers, include them in the entire blended learning campaign by:

- asking managers to do the final evaluation for employees who participated in a blend
- creating unique learning plans for managers, which include due dates, milestones, learning objectives, and learning assets
- looking for ways to publicly leverage them throughout the blend.

Small efforts to show learners their managers are invested in the program go a long way. When managers value modern learning, learners will follow suit.

Ensure Organizational Support

Gaining managerial buy-in for modern blended learning is just the first step. A broad, comprehensive, supportive learning culture is also required for improved learner performance and ongoing success.

In nontraditional learning environments, learners often face regular interruptions from co-workers, managers, and their day-to-day responsibilities. As discussed in chapter 1, there's a false, yet widespread perception that learning can be interrupted if it's not taking place in a classroom. Instructional designers need to change that perception, because frequent interruptions decrease learner retention. In addition, learner engagement will decrease if they begin to resent the process or feel obligated to complete portions of the program after working hours. Both challenges can spell disaster for the blend. Creating a supportive learning culture that treats all learning moments as "do not disturb" moments will help tremendously.

TOOL

In the blended learning environment, it is important that designers of blended learning make people accountable for their own success. Use the "Creating a Culture of Accountability for Learners" tool at the end of this chapter to create a culture of accountability for learners.

Blended Learning in the Future

When I started in L&D more than 20 years ago, I couldn't have imagined today's learning landscape. I couldn't have imagined learners accessing content using their phones.

However, I can start to imagine how learning is going to change going forward, and how that will affect blended learning.

Personalized Learning Pathways

People have always created their own personal learning paths. Every time you identify a problem that needs to be solved, you have the opportunity to identify what you need to learn, and how to learn it. You also make decisions about when you can stop learning and move on to the next thing.

Employees in your organization are doing this right now. They are using their personal networks and search engines to get the answers. As L&D becomes less of a provider of learning and more of a consultative partner, blended learning will become more and more individualized for each learner. Self-assessment and individual goals, often defined in partnership with managers, will allow learners to become more specific about their individual needs.

Your role will be to ensure that the resources necessary for learners to meet their goals are available, while also ensuring that they meet the requirements of the business. Initially, this balance between learner needs and business requirements will be difficult to maintain. But, with repeated success and refinement of the process, personalize learning pathways become more of the norm.

Experience API (xAPI)

According to Megan Torrance and Rob Houck (2017), "xAPI is a specification for how we send, store, and retrieve a wide and extensible variety of records about learning and performance experiences and subsequently share those data across platforms. These records (also known as activity statements) are sent from a variety of sources known as learning record providers or activity providers, and they are aggregated in a learning record store."

Why is xAPI powerful? Because you can track more than just interaction with e-learning courses, you can track interaction with social collaborative platforms, community networks, and human resources systems, as well as what's not usually considered part of the training purview, like help desks and document management systems. In other words, you can better track the entire learner experience.

As you learn to use xAPI, and it becomes more integrated into your existing technology infrastructure, you can start to track and assess what experiences truly engage all learners, and which ones they are actively seeking out. In five years, this experience tracking will be expected, and L&D will be using big data to make decisions about improving the experiences of your learners.

RESOURCE

In the March 2017 issue of *TD at Work*, "Making Sense of xAPI," Megan Torrance and Rob Houck offer an overview of xAPI and provide guidance to help you get started making it part of your learning management system.

Immersive Learning

Companies are using augmented reality in innovative new ways to engage customers. Do you recall the "Pokémon Go" phenomena of 2016? Within days of this augmented reality game's release, industry bloggers were envisioning the uses of this immersive experience in our learning environments. The reason that this game was so successful was that it created an authentic experience by layering media over the user's real surroundings.

There are so many potential uses for this type immersive experience in a blended learning campaign. Consider new hire nurses in a hospital setting: Over the course of their orientation, they would need to know how to fill prescriptions, where to go to pick up x-rays, and how to find the cafeteria. You could probably add a dozen items to this list without giving it much thought. Imagine if their new employee orientation included an augmented reality experience on a tablet that provided a tour of the hospital, introductions to different departments, and tips on how to be successful. This could go a long way toward reducing errors and increasing time to proficiency for new hire nurse. Adding elements of gamification could also help them interact with one another in a fun, low-risk competition.

User-Generated Content

For decades, there has been a concern about how to manage information that is leaving an organization as individuals retire or move on to other positions. To combat this "tribal knowledge" between individuals and groups that is never written down, companies began implementing knowledge management systems and processes.

Today, social collaborative tools are providing a less intrusive, and perhaps more effective, solution to the problem. Social media tools like Facebook and Twitter are teaching individuals to share user generated content. We share information about restaurants, pets, and how to take care of our gardens. As part of that sharing, interested people learn not just our opinions but nuanced knowledge that may not have been written down before. (What's the best way to sift flour when you don't own a tool? How do you tune up a 1961 Chevrolet that hasn't been started in 20 years?) Check your Internet search history. I bet you've asked similar questions. And you got answers. And since these answers were somewhere on the Internet, when other people search for the same question, they'll get similar results.

That's the power of user-generated content.

Trainingindustry.com defines user-generated content as "media content available on Internet portals and social applications that has been contributed by and for a specific community. Within the training industry, it pertains to searchable online learning content generated informally by colleagues for use by specific stakeholders of an organization."

As organizations adopt more social collaborative tools, this type of informal knowledge sharing will become more common in organizations. L&D will need to incorporate these tools into a formal blended learning design and encourage their use.

And So On

I might not be able to predict exactly what learning will look like in the future. But I do know that it will evolve. And you need to evolve with it. Look ahead. Read what experts are predicting will be important in the coming years, and plan to keep ahead of the curve. There is a lot out there. You'll need to design your own experience as well.

Design Your Personal Blended Learning Campaign

Reminder: We are all modern learners. Yes. That means you, too. There's an overwhelming amount of content, innumerable resources available for curation, and constantly emerging EdTech we can try to incorporate into our blends. Despite the expectations we feel as learning professionals, we cannot, and should not, be experts at everything.

TOOL

Use the "Learning Pathway Planning Worksheet" tool at the end of this chapter to reflect on how you will continue to develop your blended learning expertise.

As you begin to design and implement blended learning, treat the process as an opportunity for your own professional development. Create a personal learning pathway that applies the same principles you're using to support your learners. You can use a familiar framework to make your plan. For example, I've used ADDIE in my own practice:

- **Analyze.** I ask, "What do I need to learn to improve my skills? Where and when will I learn?" By asking and answering these questions, I can pick authentic treatments for each of my personal learning objectives.

- **Design.** I've found that structure and purposeful design are as mission critical to my personal learning path as they are to campaigns I've created for a client. I document learning objectives, identify measurable outcomes, and assign completion deadlines for each aspect of my personal blend.

- **Develop.** Social collaboration should be part of any blended learning initiative, including personal pathways. I make a point to develop and nurture my personal learning network to support my own professional development. I do so in two steps: I identify the experts I turn to for specific topics, and I set aside specific time for learning.

- **Implement.** Take a page out of Nike's book: Just do it. I prioritize my skill building, and honor the time I've set aside to achieve my goals. Doing so helps me better support my learners and model nontraditional learning approaches.

- **Evaluate.** I regularly take stock and ask, "Is my plan working? Do I have the right priorities based on my current projects and goals?" My direction often changes, but I make sure that it happens thoughtfully and purposefully.

PRO TIP

According to Jane Hart (2016), a personal learning network is "a network of trusted connections with whom an individual interacts (and learns from) on a regular basis." Through this network, you'll make connections and grow relationships with those who have different areas of expertise. As you collaborate, you exchange insights, answer questions, and discuss the goings-on in this new learning environment. This will allow you to stay on top of trends, identifying and accessing key information. You'll also swap ideas and expand on what you learned on your own. It means you'll have a collection of people to turn to when a challenging or ambiguous concept arises, letting you focus on getting an answer, rather than worrying about where to start.

Create a Personal Curation Practice

Chapter 3 discussed the role of curation in the design of blended learning campaigns. Generally, when thinking about curation for the learning field, it relates to an expert commenting on content and sharing it with the field. You should start curation on a personal level, but with so much rich information being delivered by your personal learning network (PLN), how can you organize it?

Everyone has a personal way of managing content overload. This is what I do with that folder full of articles, webinar recordings, and newsletters that I plan to read one day:

- I delete anything I've been holding onto for more than 14 days. There is too much information coming in for me to worry about what I have ignored for weeks already.
- I consider why I thought items were important in the first place. Were they colleague recommendations? Did keywords stand out?
- I create email rules to organize the content, and schedule time every week to review resources by sender. When I find myself deleting everything from a source, I unsubscribe.
- Instead of investing hours in watching webinar recordings, I look for more accessible microlearning resources like articles, blogs, and infographics from the same source.

PRO TIP

If you can't capture even one note on why an item is important, discard it. It won't suddenly become important six months from now, because you won't remember it existed. If you do decide you need to retrieve lost information, it's only a search engine away.

As our roles and responsibilities expand, our time becomes more limited and more precious. Devoting time to cultivating our personal learning networks (PLNs) can feel luxurious. It's also commonplace to feel like we have nothing meaningful to contribute to these robust learning communities.

We must make time for social collaboration. By identifying helpful content, curating useful resources, and sharing insights, you add value to the different parts of your personal learning network. Social networks like Twitter and LinkedIn are a great place to begin the process.

Contributing to your PLN enhances your personal learning experience by:

- Encouraging reciprocation—When you share your expertise, your network is more likely to share as well.
- Skill building through teaching—Solidify your new knowledge by sharing it with others.
- Growing your network—PLNs are worth your time and attention, and increased engagement equals more resources and advice.

My best practices for giving back to a personal learning network include sharing content and giving credit where it's due, answering questions and responding to discussions, and recognizing members of my PLN who've helped me. Remember, what you give is what you get when it comes to building a network.

TOOL

Need help getting started? Refer to this list of industry experts in the tool "Creating Your Personal Learning Network" at the end of this chapter to determine whom you should include in your personal learning network.

Final Thoughts

To be successful as a learning experience architect in this modern learning landscape, you need to do more than stand and deliver. You need to be able to partner with your learners and with the business to meet the needs of both groups. You need to make decisions about how to sequence content, while also including instructional strategies, techniques, and technologies in your design discussions.

Every decision you make will affect the perception of blended learning in your organization. Start simply: Develop a strong design plan, and document everything. This will create the blueprint for your future initiatives, and establish you as an expert in the field.

As you look ahead, blended learning campaigns will be commonplace—the right content, in the right place, at the right time, for the right audience. After a while, you'll wonder how you taught and learned before.

Questions to Explore

- What communication vehicles do you have that you can use to promote blended learning?
- What incentives exist or can you implement to engage managers in blended learning initiatives?
- What data would help you make decisions about blended learning design if they were easily accessible?
- If technology and budget weren't barriers, what types of immersive experiences could help your learners?
- What is your plan to continue building your skillset in modern blended learning?
- What do you imagine the future of blended learning looks like?

Tools for Support

Blended Learning Marketing Plan Worksheet

In today's networked world, word gets around fast. Make sure the word about blended learning is positive, and constantly being reinforced. An initial marketing burst without continuing effort will make your initiative seem like another passing fad. Regular news about what campaigns are coming up, and their importance to the organization, will help employees understand that blended learning is an integral part of the organization's learning culture. If blended learning is "in," employees will demand to be part of the action.

Use these tips and the communication plan template to create your marketing plan and organize your marketing schedule.

- Make the "What's in it for me?" message loud and clear. Provide information about why and how the training will benefit the learners. Use testimonials or schedule an informational meeting so interested learners can come and ask questions about the value blended learning offers.
- Ask learners for testimonials immediately after training—make it part of the evaluation form. It is important to capture positive comments about the blended learning experience when emotions and satisfaction are high.
- Use the company intranet, emails, and bulletin boards to market the benefits of online learning. Keep this communication going so that it doesn't lose its potency.
- Use blended learning to teach about blended learning. Set up an orientation meeting within the platform so people can see what to expect and how blended learning works. Provide instructions and guidelines so potential learners also can see how communication will work during a course. Advertise the orientation as a "sneak peek" of what's to come. Keep the session short and schedule it at a quiet time in your organization. You can also record the orientation for on-demand playback.
- Get your subject matter experts to help you spread the word about the online learning initiative. Keep in touch with people who are excited about virtual training, and ask them to share their experiences with other departments,

supervisors, and employees. Remember—word of mouth is one of the most powerful ways to spread the news.

- Create a theme or campaign for your blended learning initiative. Creative use of posters, email, social media, fun fonts, colors, and logos can keep your campaign exciting. Keep the campaign organized and on a regular schedule.

- Send a weekly or monthly email. Make sure the subject line of the email is attention grabbing, so it does not get lost in overfull inboxes. You should also send out regular updates to your internal social media sites.

- Include a survey about potential training programs as part of your marketing campaign to identify hot button, unclear, or very popular issues. Feedback will help you learn what is and isn't working.

- Get the company newsletter to dedicate a specific section to blended learning. Post regular updates, events, and milestones so that they can be shared with all employees, even while the course is still going on.

- Create a brand for your blended learning initiative. Design a logo and put it on everything you distribute, including workbooks, do-not-disturb signs, certificates of completion, and maybe even facilitator T-shirts.

Date	Targeted Audience	Message or Event	Method or Media	Who Delivers	Notes
May 13	Learners	Learn about blended learning!	Video about the "WIIFM"	Popular facilitator	TD develops material

Creating a Culture of Accountability for Learners

In the blended learning environment, it is important that designers of blended learning make people accountable for their own success. The onus is on the learner to be responsible for their learning in this environment. It's not enough to expect that people will be responsible; you must reinforce that expectation through your own behaviors.

According to the Society for Human Resource Management, there are six steps to creating a culture of accountability in the workplace (Pennington 2015). They apply to blended learning campaigns as well. In creating a culture of accountability for your learners, you set them up for the most successful blended learning experience.

Set and communicate clear expectations.

- Outline individual learning pathways, and share them in a course map that includes context, order, and the amount of time it will take to complete each activity and lesson. Be clear about what is required and what might be optional, and provide up-front guidance on what it means to "complete" the experience.
- Establish and publish a set of ground rules regarding how learners should behave while participating. Include information that will help them understand what is expected of them. And don't forget to include some type of checklist they can use beforehand so they are ready and prepared for each lesson.

Align individual and team goals with the departmental and organizational strategies and vision.

- Design exercises that allow learners to apply to real world situations and solve real business problems. They are more immediately relatable than case studies, and will also be useful in the future when learners want additional practice outside the formal learning campaign.
- Include an activity that allows learners to customize their own personal learning paths based on what they have learned and what they identify as personal development gaps.

Provide time, training, tools, and resources.

- Create an orientation to the blended learning experience. Blended learning is a new and mysterious (and often intimidating) experience for many individuals. A playful and fun "let's get to know what blended learning is all about" orientation will go a long way toward creating an organization that embraces blended learning as a regular course of business.

- Include microlearning tools as part of the design as a foundation for future and perpetual learning, so learners can quickly retrieve and recall this information in a critical moment of need.

Empower people to succeed.

- Provide a manager orientation to blended learning so managers can participate in the experience and understand the importance of the time commitment required of learners.

Provide recognition and feedback.

- Develop a gamified incentive plan awarding points to your learners based on their accomplishments. Set out your objectives and link them to the point system. At the end of the learning campaign, participants can redeem their points for a digital badge to recognize learning accomplishments.

Act when individuals and teams do not meet expectations.

- Encourage learners to take charge of their experiences by doing things like fixing technical problems with local support, instead of relying on the facilitator or producer to fix them.

- Encourage learners to seek their own answers instead of just providing content. You may need to direct them to where to find the answer. For instance, if someone says, "I'm going to miss the next session, how do I access the recording?" say, "On the course home page you'll find instructions for accessing all recordings." Or if they say, "I didn't get that video," say, "all resources are on the course map, through this link." It is your job as the learning experience architect to teach the learners to fish, not just to feed them the fish, as the saying goes. Learners in the virtual environment must take the responsibility to be successful.

Learning Pathway Planning Worksheet

Use the questions in this worksheet to help plan and guide your own learning pathways.

1. What are your personal learning goals?

2. What resources will you use to achieve your personal learning goals?

3. What networks will you tap into to achieve your personal learning goals?

4. What might get in the way of achieving your goals along your personal learning pathway?

5. What can you do to ensure these barriers don't prevent you from progressing?

6. How will you reward yourself when you achieve your goals and reach milestones along your learning pathway?

Creating Your Personal Learning Network

There are many qualified experts in the talent development field. This list represents members of my personal learning network, and are my go-to experts for all things learning related. Review the resources, and use them to kick start your personal learning network. Who else would you add to your list?

Gamification and Game-Based Learning

Karl Kapp (@kkapp)

- Books and Articles
    - » *The Gamification of Learning and Instruction*
    - » *Gadgets, Games and Gizmos for Learning*
    - » "Game-Based Learning Methods and Strategies" (https://game-learn .com/game-based-learning-methods-strategies-karl-kapp)
- Other
    - » Official Website: http://karlkapp.com
    - » Podcast: "Exploring Gamification and Learning with Karl Kapp" (www.leadinglearning.com/gamification-learning-karl-kapp)

Social Learning

Jane Bozarth (@janebozarth)

- Books and Articles
    - » *Social Media for Trainers*
    - » "From Traditional ID to ID 2.0" (www.td.org/magazines/td-magazine /from-traditional-instruction-to-instructional-design-20)
    - » "Nuts and Bolts: Social Media for Learning" (www.learningsolutionsmag .com/articles/762/nuts-and-bolts-social-media-for-learning)
- Other
    - » Webinar: "Social Learning" (https://vimeo.com/25062639)
    - » Podcast: "Using Social Media for Learning: A Conversation With Jane Bozarth" (http://theelearningcoach.com/podcasts/2)

Modern Workplace Learning

Jane Hart (@C4LPT)

- Books and Articles
  - » *Modern Workplace Learning: A Resource Book for L&D*
  - » "Modern Professional Learning: Guidelines & Resources" (http://modernworkplacelearning.com/magazine/modern-professional-learning-guidelines-resources)
  - » "20 Ways to Prepare Yourself for Modern Workplace Learning" (http://internettimealliance.com/wp/2016/04/20/20-ways-to-prepare-yourself-for-modern-workplace-learning)
- Other
  - » Official Website: http://janehart.com
  - » Blog: www.c4lpt.co.uk/blog
  - » Presentation: "Learning in the Modern Workplace: Moving Beyond E-Learning" (www.slideshare.net/janehart/learning-in-the-modern-workplace-43899391)

xAPI

Megan Torrance (@MMTorrance)

- Articles and *TD at Work* issues
  - » "Making Sense of xAPI" (March 2017 *TD at Work*)
  - » "Getting Started With xAPI: Take a Hike With an Expert" (www.learningsolutionsmag.com/articles/2295/getting-started-with-xapi-take-a-hike-with-an-expert)
  - » "17 Things You Can Do (Better) With xAPI Than With SCORM" (www.td.org/insights/17-things-you-can-do-better-with-xapi-than-with-scorm)
- Other
  - » Official Website: www.torrancelearning.com
  - » Interview: "xAPI Gaining Traction: An Interview With Megan Torrance" (www.webcourseworks.com/xapi-gaining-traction-an-interview-with-megan-torrance)

Global Learning

Laura Overton (@lauraoverton)

- Article
  - » "Global Learning: Sharing Opportunities and Challenges" (https://towardsmaturity.org/2015/10/01/global-learning-sharing-opportunities-and-challenges)
- Other
  - » Official Website: https://towardsmaturity.org
  - » Slideshare: "Building a Global Learning Culture" (https://towardsmaturity.org/2016/02/01/building-a-global-learning-culture)

Virtual Teams

Brenda Huettner (@bphuettner)

- Books and Chapters
  - » *Managing Virtual Teams: Getting the Most From Wikis, Blogs, and Other Collaborative Tools*
  - » "Choosing Online Collaborative Tools" (Chapter 6 in *Virtual Teamwork*)
- Other
  - » Official Website: http://p-ndesigns.com

Microlearning

Ray Jimenez (@RayJimenez)

- Articles
  - » "Breaking Ten Rules Using Microlearning" (http://vignettestraining.blogspot.com/2016/09/breaking-10-training-rules-using-micro.html)
  - » "Are You Ready for Microlearning Jobs?" (http://vignettestraining.blogspot.com/2017/05/hands-on-5-are-you-ready-for-micro.html)
  - » "Why Does Microlearning Mean Better Learning?" (http://vignettestraining.blogspot.com/2017/04/why-does-micro-learning-mean-better.html)
- Other
  - » Official Website: www.vignetteslearning.com
  - » Webinar: "elearnChat151: Dr. Ray Jimenez on MicroLearning" (https://vimeo.com/117421993)

Learning Strategy

JD Dillon (@JD_Dillon

- Articles
    - » "Curated Insights: Why Knowledge Sharing at Work Is a Good Thing" (https://axonify.com/blog/curated-insights-knowledge-sharing-work-good-thing)
    - » "Learning in Layers" (www.td.org/magazines/td-magazine/learning-in-layers)
    - » "10 Symptoms of an Unhealthy Learning System" (www.mimeo.com/blog/10-symptoms-unhealthy-learning-ecosystem)
- Other
    - » Interview: "LearningToGo Podcast: Axonify Principle Learning Strategist JD Dillon" (www.youtube.com/watch?v=V-PkSLvr6Kc)

Learning Management Systems

Michael Feldstein (@mfeldstein67)

- Articles
    - » "Who's Really to Blame for the Failures of our Learning Management Systems?" (www.chronicle.com/article/What-s-Really-to-Blame-for/235620t)
    - » "Dammit, the LMS" (http://mfeldstein.com/dammit-lms)
- Other
    - » Official Website: http://mfeldstein.com

The Future of Learning

Bryan Alexander (@BryanAlexander)

- Books and Articles
    - » *The New Digital Storytelling*
    - » "Future Trends in Technology and Education" (https://bryanalexander.org/future-trends-in-technology-and-education)
- Other
    - » Official Website: https://bryanalexander.org
    - » Interview: "UpTechTalk: Future of Learning 1: Bryan Alexander" (www.podparadise.com/Podcast/947956503/Listen/1472672550/0)

Research

Josh Bersin (@Josh_Bersin)

- Articles
    - » "The Disruption of Digital Learning: Ten Things We Have Learned" (http://joshbersin.com/2017/03/the-disruption-of-digital-learning-ten-things-we-have-learned)
    - » "Watch Out Corporate Learning, Here Comes Disruption" (www.forbes.com/sites/joshbersin/2017/03/28/watch-out-corporate-learning-here-comes-disruption/#6f0a7187dc59)
    - » "How Do You Define Digital Learning?" (www.clomedia.com/2017/06/11/define-digital-learning)
- Other
    - » Official Website: http://joshbersin.com

Virtual and Augmented Reality

Monica Burns (@classtechtips)

- Books and Articles
    - » *Deeper Learning With QR Codes and Augmented Reality*
    - » "A Virtual Reality Tool for Your Classroom" (www.simplek12.com/3-minute-problem-solver/virtual-reality-tool-classroom)
- Other
    - » Official Website: www.classtechtips.com
    - » Podcast: "The Ed Tech Podcast: #21 With Monica Burns" (https://theedtechpodcast.libsyn.com/21-with-monica-burns-classtechtips com-with-guest-appearance-from-ron-reed-executive-producer-sxsw-edu)
    - » Interview: "QR Codes in the Classroom: An Interview With Monica Burns" (www.ictineducation.org/home-page/qr-codes-in-the-classroom-an-interview-with-monica-burns)

Curation

Stephen Walsh (@AndersPink)

- Books and Articles
    - » *Content Curation for Learning*
    - » "Continuous Curated Learning: The Business Case" (http://modernworkplacelearning.com/magazine/author/stephen)
    - » "5 Ways to Personalize Learning With Curated Content" (www.ht2labs.com/blog/5-ways-to-personalise-learning-with-curated-content)
- Other
    - » Official Website: https://anderspink.com
    - » Interview: "Curation and the Cloud" (www.youtube.com/watch?v=VRaNHbKBPso)

Data Driven Learning

Phil Ice (@technostats)

- Articles and Papers
    - » "Data Changes Everything: Delivering on the Promise of Learning Analytics in Higher Education" (http://er.educause.edu/articles/2012/7/data-changes-everything-delivering-on-the-promise-of-learning-analytics-in-higher-education)
    - » "Introduction to Analytics for E-Learning" (www.learntechlib.org/p/38789)
    - » "Using the Community of Inquiry Framework to Inform Effective Instructional Design" (www.researchgate.net/publication/287234577_Using_the_Community_of_Inquiry_Framework_to_Inform_Effective_Instructional_Design)

Additional Resources

Hart, J. 2016. "The Future of Work and Learning 1: The Professional Ecosystem." Internet Time Alliance blog, May 8. http://internettimealliance.com/wp/2016/05/08/the-future-of-work-and-learning-1-the-professional-ecosystem.

Kim, D.M., and C. Choi. 2004. "Developing Future Leaders at Hyundai Motor Company Through Blended Learning." *Industrial and Commercial Training* 36(7): 286-90.

Pennington, R. 2015. "Building a Culture of Accountability." *HR Magazine*, September 1. www.shrm.org/hr-today/news/hr-magazine/pages/0915-building-an-accountable-culture.aspx.

Rainie, L., and J. Anderson. 2017. *The Future of Jobs and Job Training.* Washington, D.C.: Pew Research Center. www.pewinternet.org/2017/05/03/the-future-of-jobs-and-jobs-training.

Torrance, M., and R. Houck. 2017. "Making Sense of xAPI." *TD at Work*, March. Alexandria, VA: ATD Press.

Training Industry. 2013. "User-Generated Content." Content Development, November 5. www.trainingindustry.com/wiki/user-generated-content.

Acknowledgments

The blended learning campaign model evolved, and continues to evolve, as a result of the efforts of the InSync Blended Learning Hub Team: Phylise Banner, Kristin Kernan, Michele Israel, Cathy Smith, Karin Rex, and Jenna Cooper. The effort was worth it. Thanks also to Chip Dye, for seeing value in the idea; Katelind Hays for ensuring this book was a quality product; and Erika Melmed and Vickie Hadge for keeping it all working.

About the Author

Jennifer Hofmann, virtual classroom mastermind and blended learning pioneer, is founder and president of InSync Training. Her entirely virtual consulting firm specializes in the design and delivery of engaging, innovative, and effective modern blended learning. Under her expert leadership, Inc. 500|5000 named InSync Training the 10th fastest-growing education company in the United States in 2013 and the 20th fastest in 2014, and inducted it to its Inc. 5000 list for four consecutive years. Dell Women's Entrepreneur Network, *Forbes* Most Powerful Women Issue, The NativeAdVantage, and Goldman Sachs 10,000 Small Businesses have all recognized Jennifer's entrepreneurial drive.

Jennifer has written and contributed to a number of well-received and highly regarded books, including *The Synchronous Trainer's Survival Guide: Facilitating Successful Live Online Courses, Meetings, and Events; Live and Online!: Tips, Techniques, and Ready to Use Activities for the Virtual Classroom;* and *Tailored Learning: Designing the Blend That Fits.*

Jennifer frequently presents in person and online for leading learning organizations, including the Training Magazine Network, ATD, the eLearning Guild, and Citrix. Subscribe to Jennifer's blog at blog.insynctraining.com and connect with her on LinkedIn for new content and timely insights.

Index